EASY PIANO SONGS

FOR BEGINNERS

SIMPLE SHEET MUSIC OF FAMOUS FAVORITES

COLLECTED AND ARRANGED BY
ANGELA MARSHALL

Easy Piano Songs for Beginners

Simple Sheet Music of Famous Favorites

ISBN: 9798806193958

Published by Avanell Publishing Inc

www.avanellpublishing.com

Bonus Downloads

This book includes free digital content.
Visit **www.avanellpublishing.com** or scan the QR code below
to access your bonus materials,

- Fully orchestrated recordings of each song

- Printable reference charts to use while you play

- Lessons and charts for left hand playing

- Practice tips to help you build your skills

- Sheet music of additional songs

Table of Contents

Table of Contents

How to Read Piano Music

A B C D E F G

Piano keys are named after the letters of the alphabet, but they only go to G!

The piano has black and white keys.
The black keys are arranged in groups of 2 and 3.

The letters **C D E**
are by a group of 2.

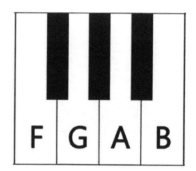

The letters **F G A B**
are by a group of 3.

The pattern of 2 and 3 repeats across the keyboard.
Use the groups of black keys to find the right notes on the piano.

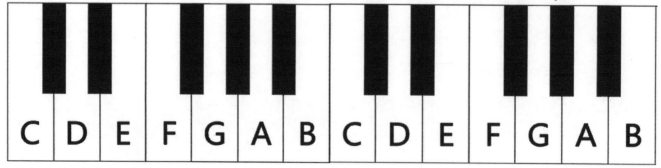

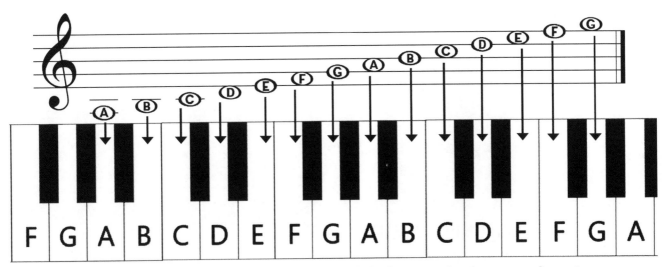

Each note is a letter of the musical alphabet and a key on the piano.

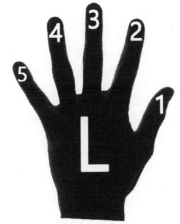

Each finger has a number.
Thumbs are number one!

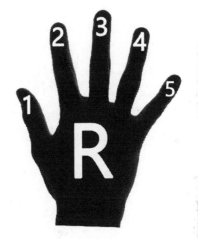

Each type of note gets a different number of beats.

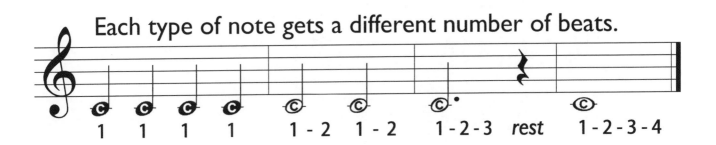

1   1   1   1   1 - 2   1 - 2   1 - 2 - 3   *rest*   1 - 2 - 3 - 4

Level One

The songs in Level One only use five notes.

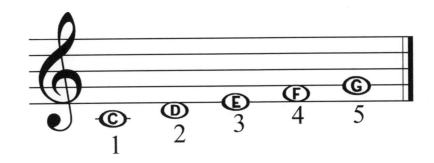

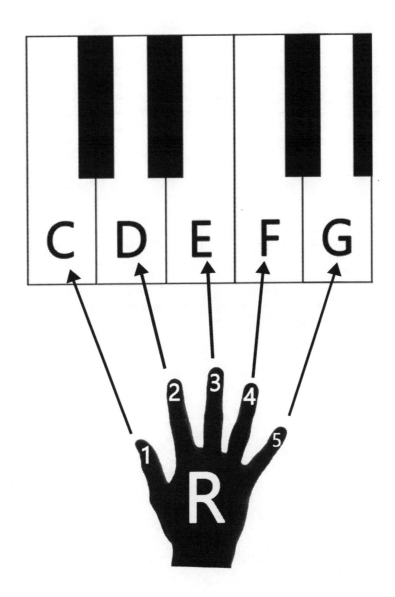

Mary Had a Little Lamb

American Folk Song

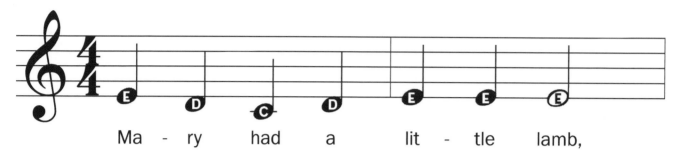

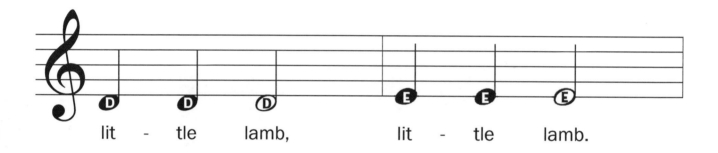

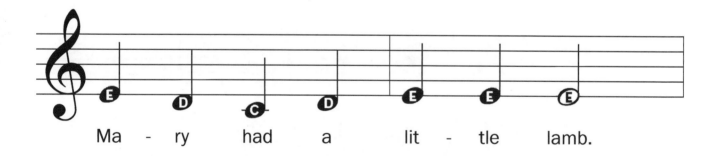

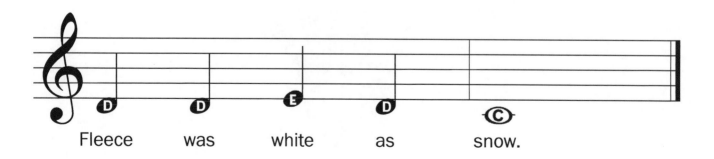

Hot Cross Buns

English Folk Song

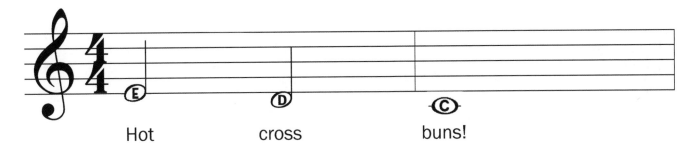

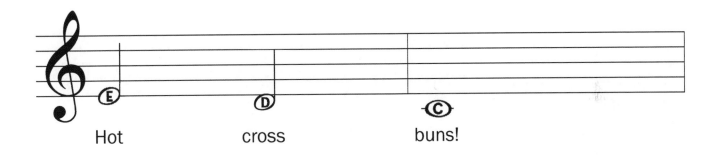

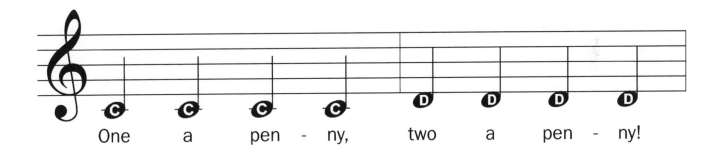

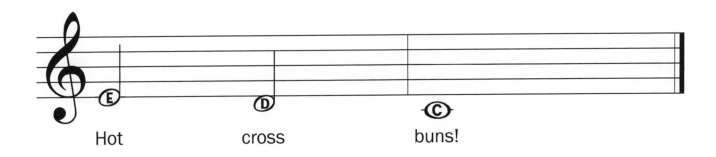

Au Clair de la Lune

French Folk Song

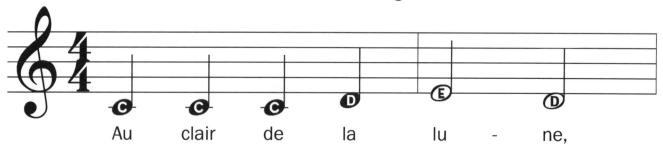

Au   clair   de   la   lu - ne,

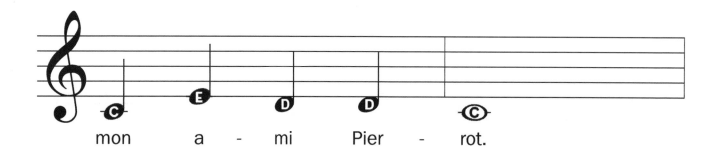

mon   a - mi   Pier - rot.

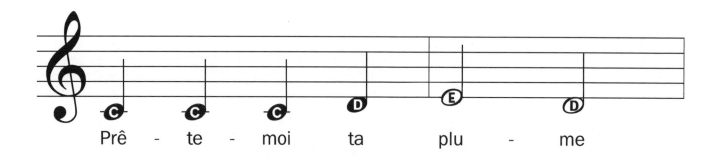

Prê - te - moi   ta   plu - me

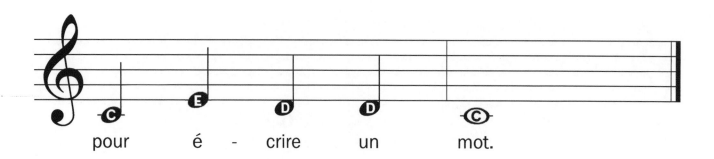

pour   é - crire   un   mot.

Translation
By the light of the moon, my friend Pierrot,
Lend me your pen to write a word.

Ode to Joy

Ludwig van Beethoven

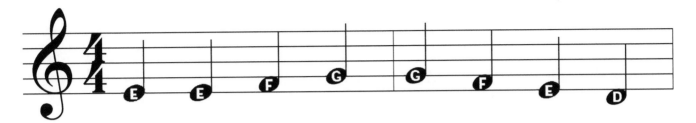

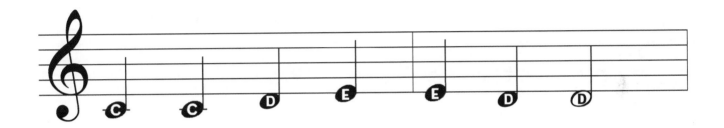

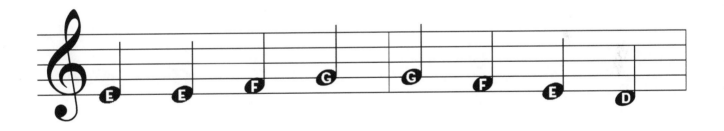

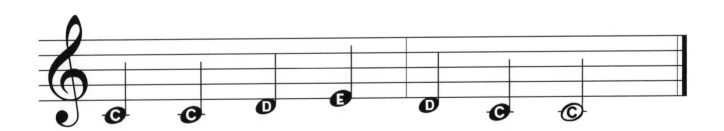

Go Tell Aunt Rhody

American Folk Song

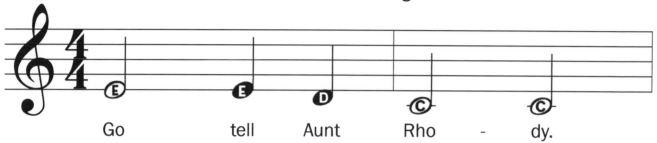

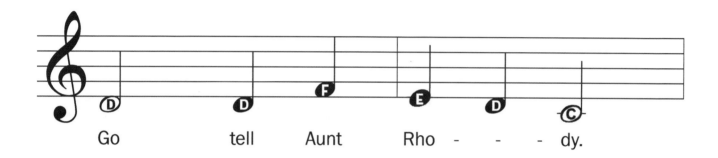

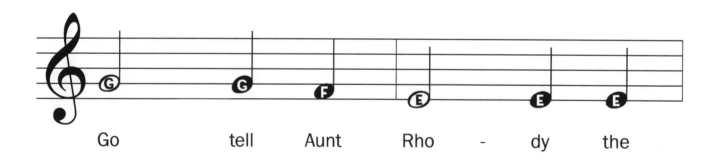

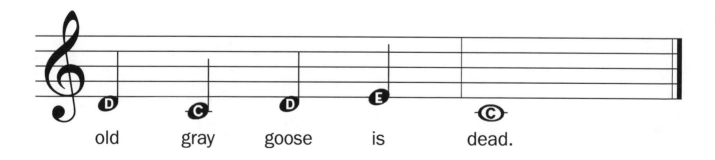

Aura Lea

W. W. Fosdick and George R. Poulton

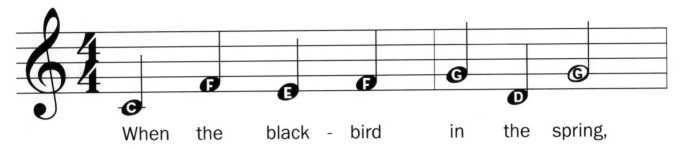

When the black - bird in the spring,

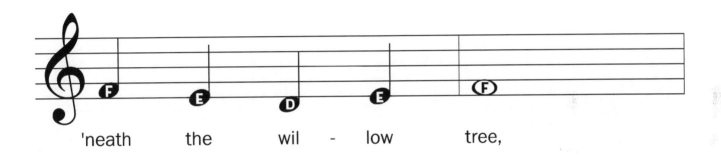

'neath the wil - low tree,

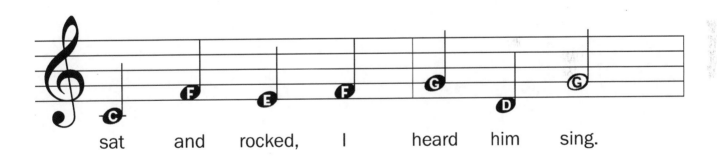

sat and rocked, I heard him sing.

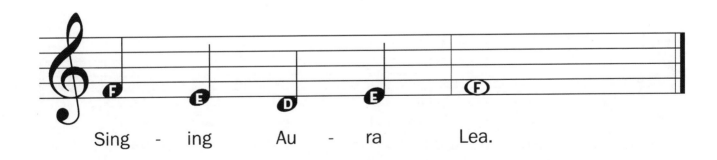

Sing - ing Au - ra Lea.

Famous Favorite
Elvis Presley used the tune of "Aura Lea"
for his 1956 hit song "Love Me Tender."

Good King Wenceslas

Traditional Christmas Carol

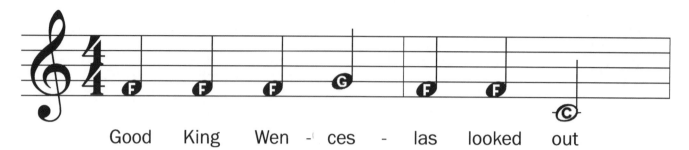

Good King Wen - ces - las looked out

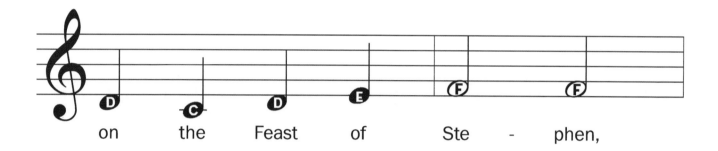

on the Feast of Ste - phen,

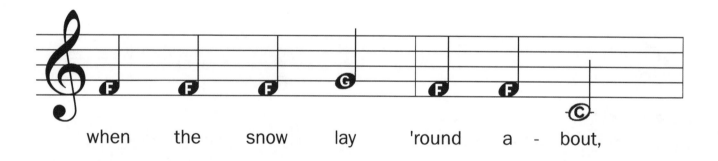

when the snow lay 'round a - bout,

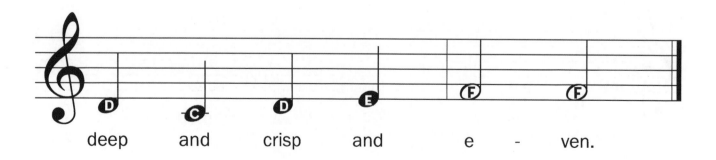

deep and crisp and e - ven.

Hallelujah Chorus

George Frideric Handel

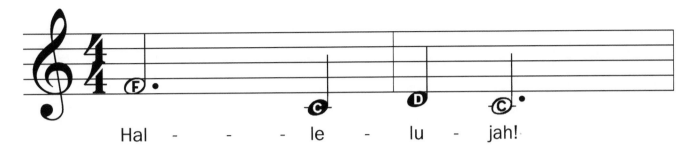

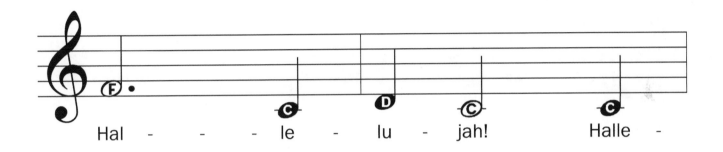

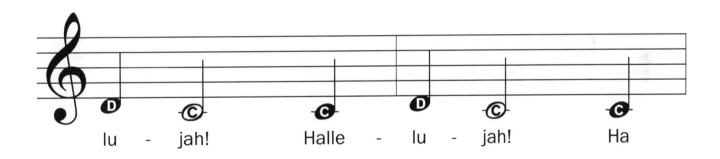

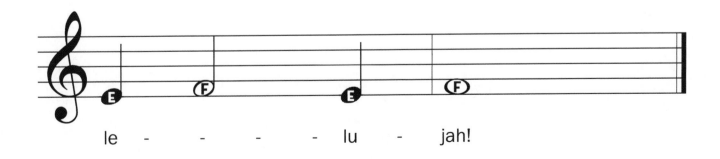

Largo from New World Symphony

Antonín Dvořák

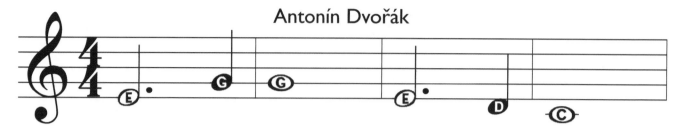

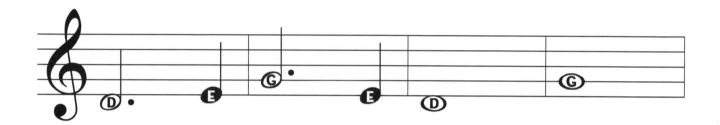

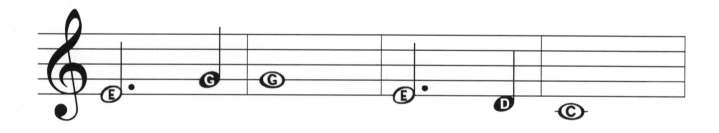

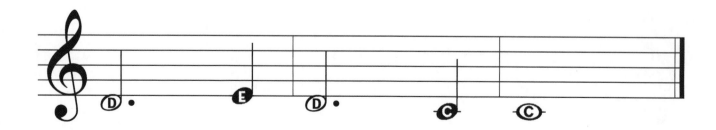

The Dreidel Song

Traditional Hanukkah Song

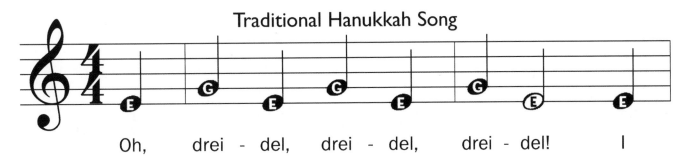

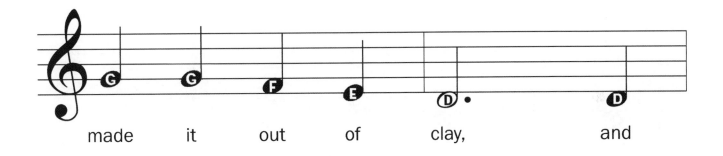

Oh, drei - del, drei - del, drei - del! I

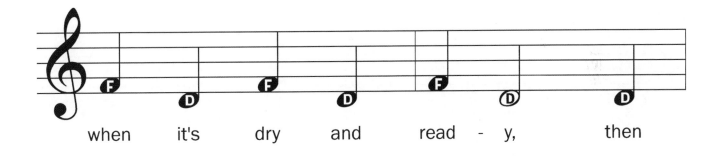

made it out of clay, and

when it's dry and read - y, then

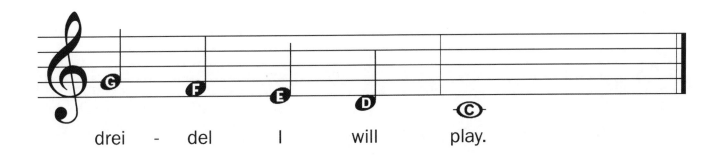

drei - del I will play.

Itsy Bitsy Spider

American Folk Song

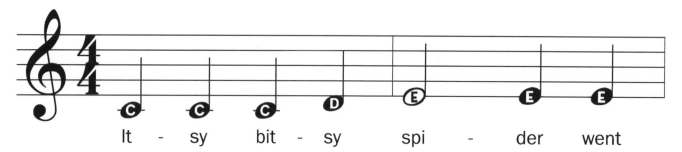

It - sy bit - sy spi - der went

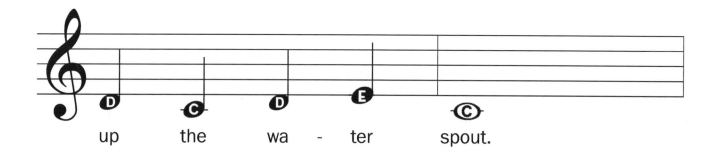

up the wa - ter spout.

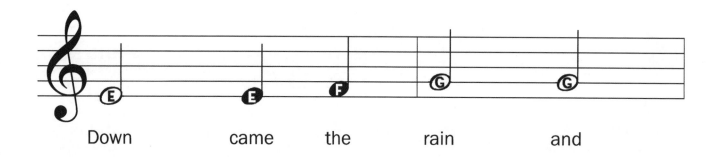

Down came the rain and

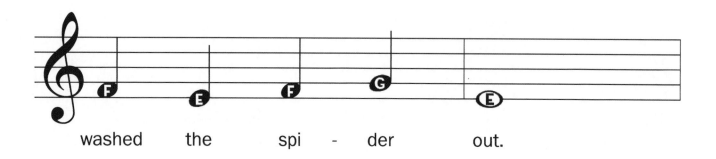

washed the spi - der out.

Itsy Bitsy Spider

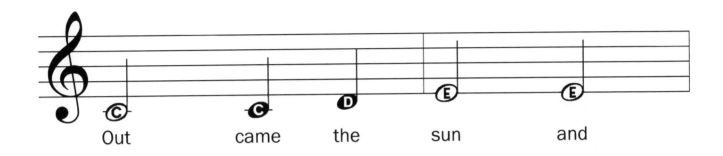

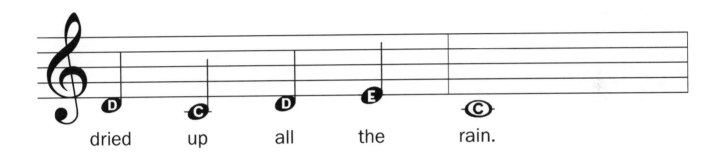

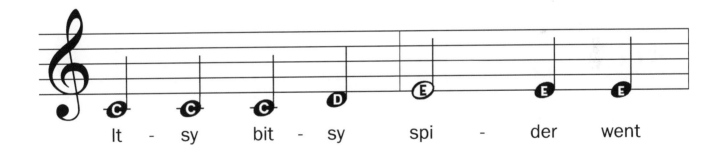

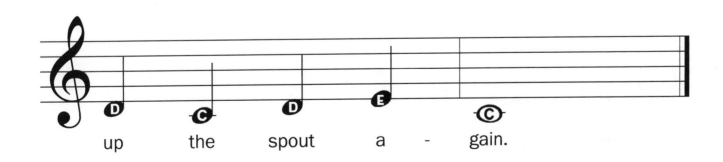

Lightly Row

American Folk Song from German Melody

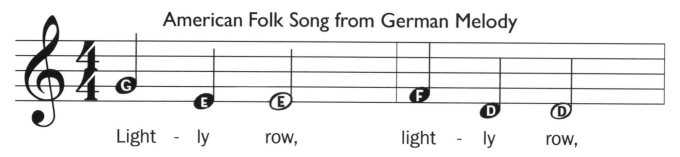

Light - ly   row,   light - ly   row,

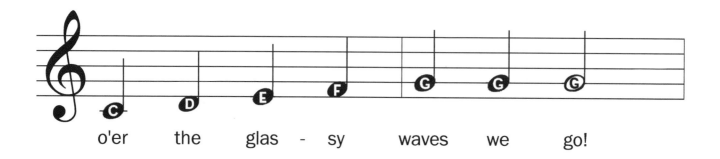

o'er   the   glas - sy   waves   we   go!

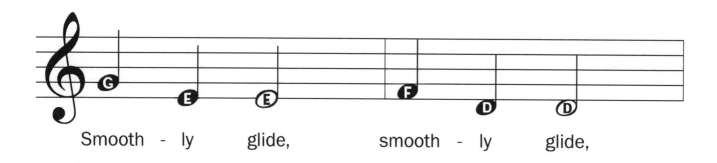

Smooth - ly   glide,   smooth - ly   glide,

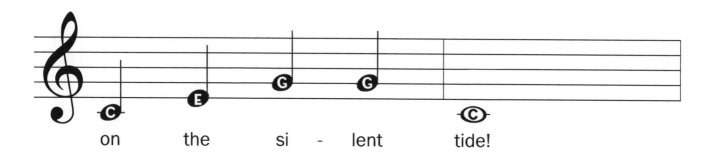

on   the   si - lent   tide!

Lightly Row

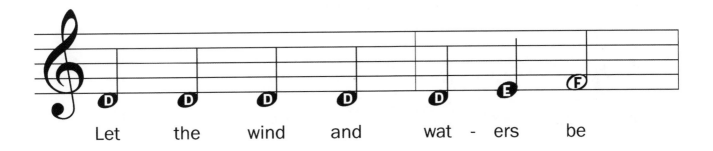

Let the wind and wat - ers be

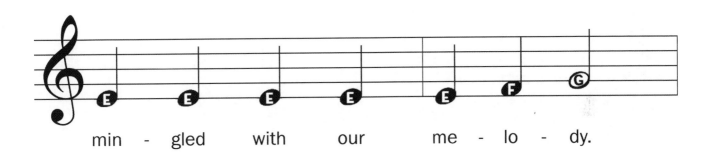

min - gled with our me - lo - dy.

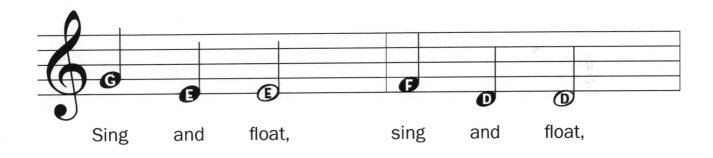

Sing and float, sing and float,

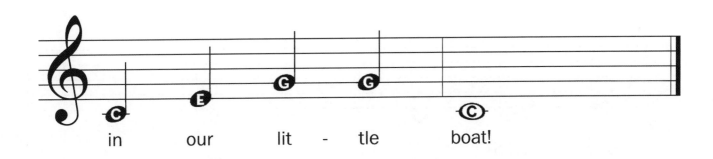

in our lit - tle boat!

Jingle Bells

James Pierpont

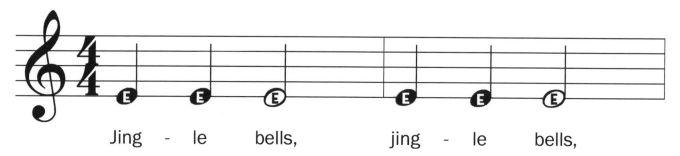

Jing - le bells, jing - le bells,

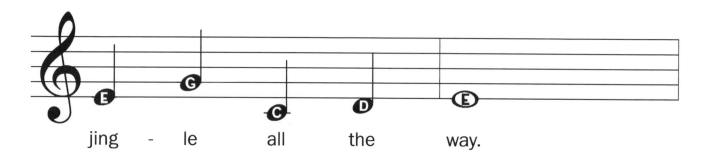

jing - le all the way.

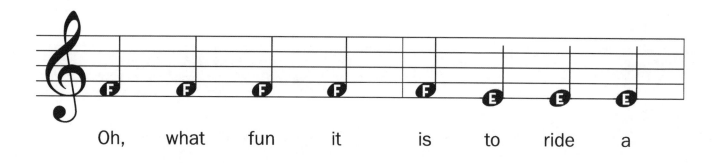

Oh, what fun it is to ride a

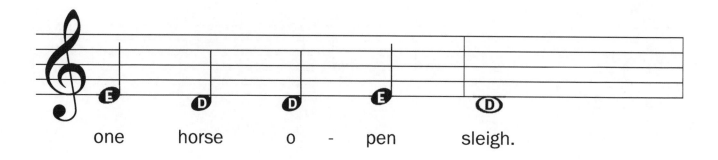

one horse o - pen sleigh.

Jingle Bells

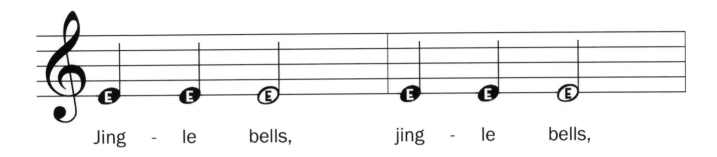

Jing - le bells, jing - le bells,

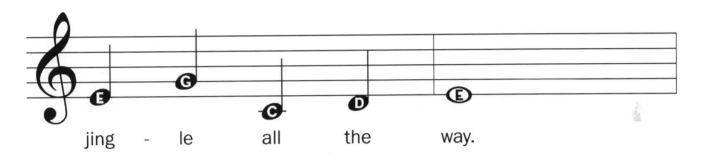

jing - le all the way.

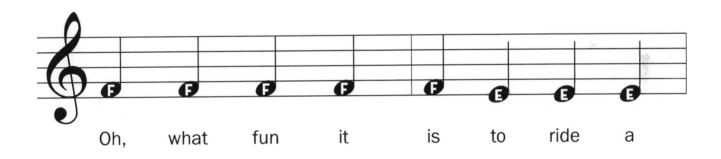

Oh, what fun it is to ride a

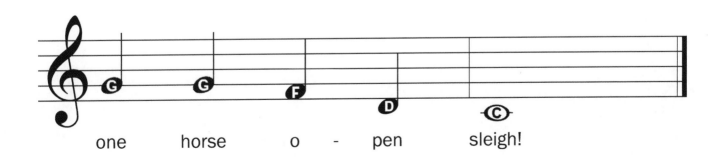

one horse o - pen sleigh!

When the Saints Go Marching In

African American Spiritual

Oh,   when   the   saints!

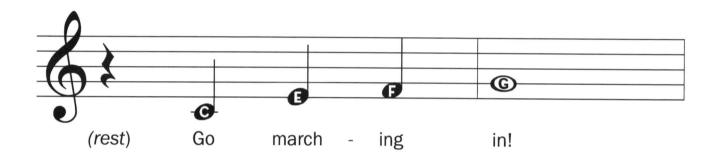

(rest)   Go   march -   ing   in!

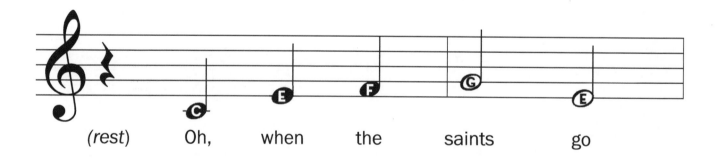

(rest)   Oh,   when   the   saints   go

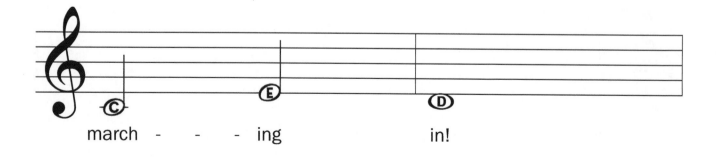

march - - - ing   in!

When the Saints Go Marching In

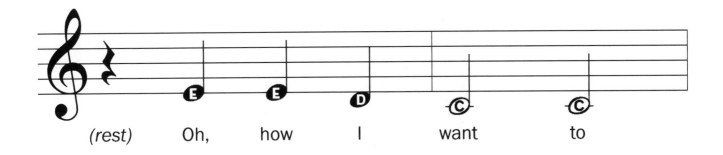

(rest)   Oh,   how   I   want   to

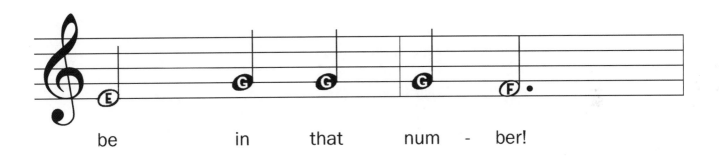

be   in   that   num - ber!

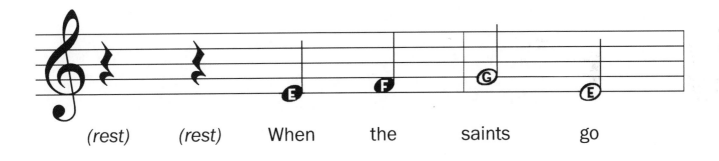

(rest)   (rest)   When   the   saints   go

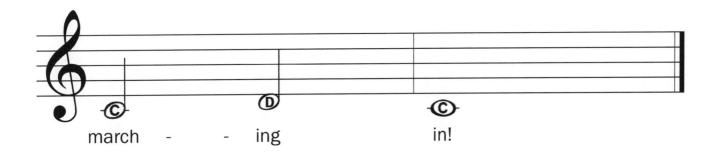

march - - ing   in!

Level Two

The songs in Level Two add two notes.

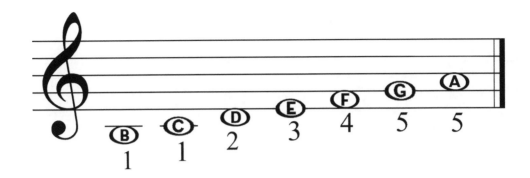

Move fingers one and five to the side to reach the new notes.

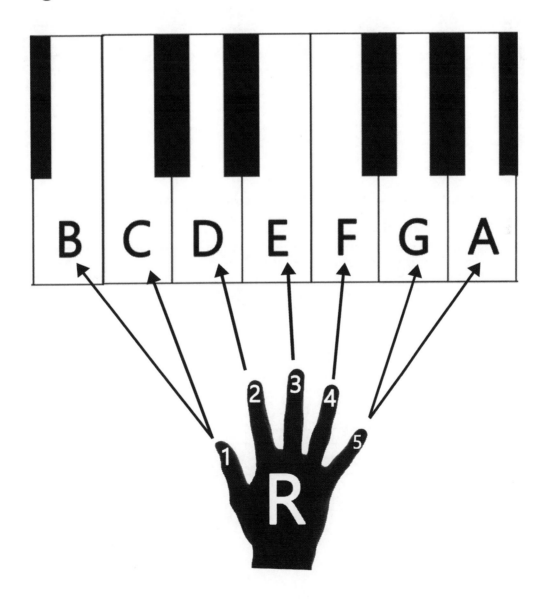

Rain, Rain, Go Away

English Folk Song

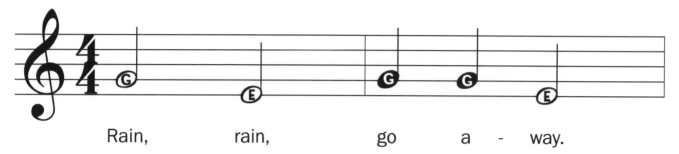

Rain,   rain,   go a - way.

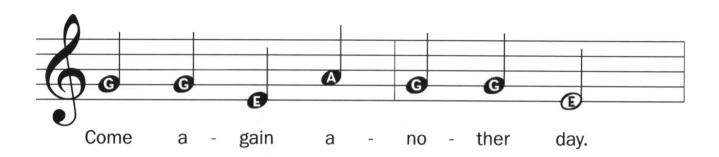

Come a - gain a - no - ther day.

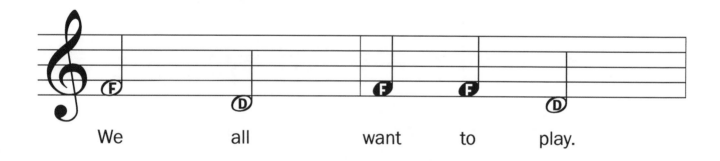

We all want to play.

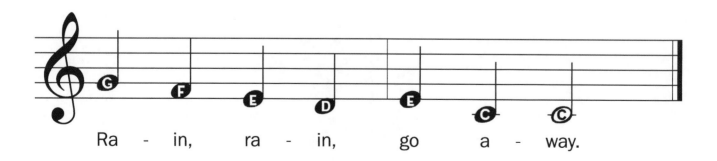

Ra - in, ra - in, go a - way.

London Bridge is Falling Down

English Folk Song

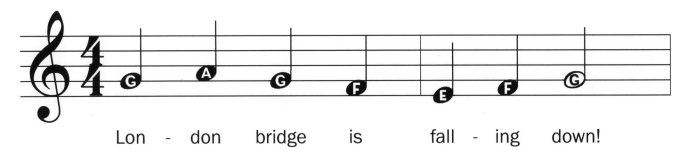

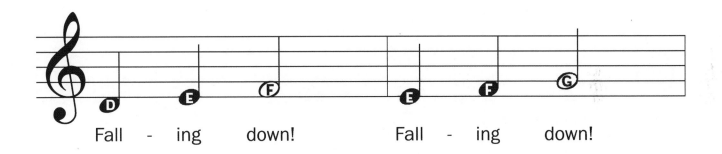

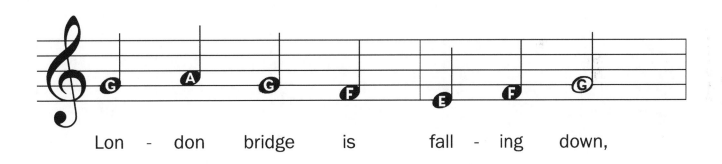

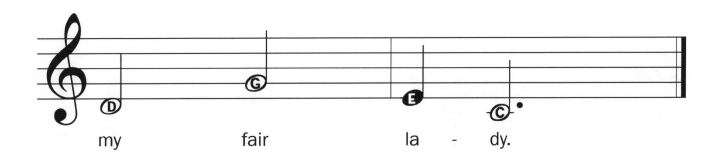

Deck the Hall

Welsh Christmas Carol

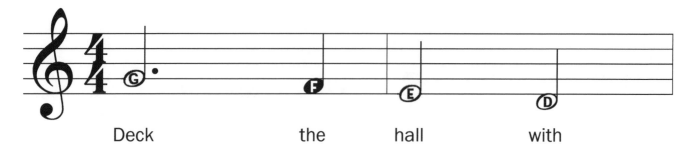

Deck the hall with

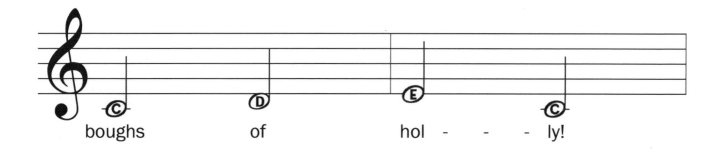

boughs of hol - - - ly!

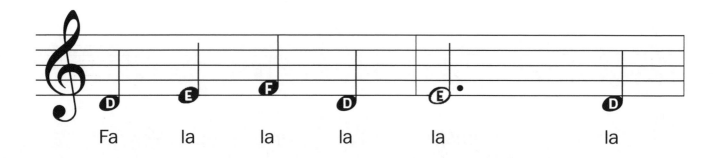

Fa la la la la la

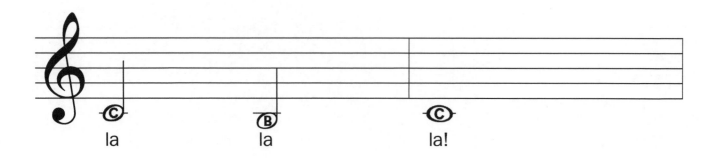

la la la!

Deck the Hall

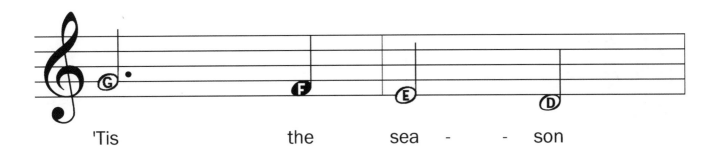

'Tis   the   sea - - son

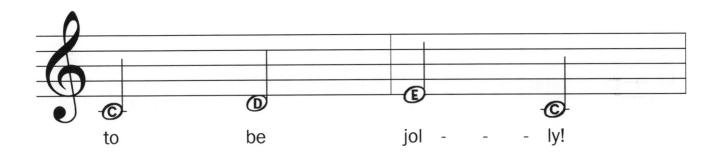

to   be   jol - - - ly!

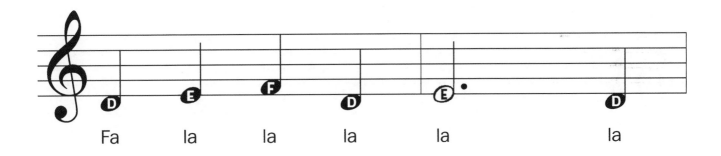

Fa   la   la   la   la   la

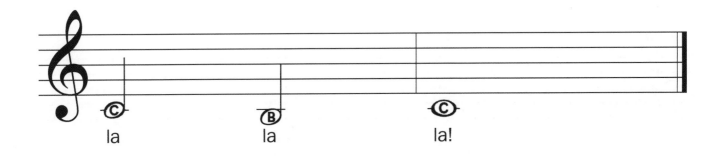

la   la   la!

Ring Around the Rosie

English Folk Song

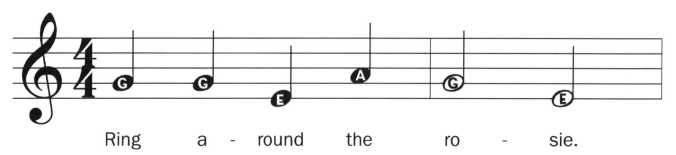

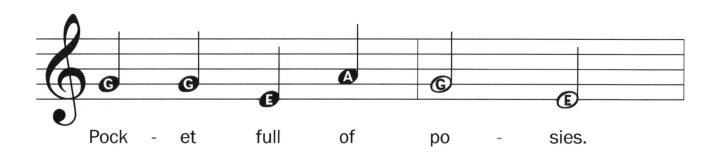

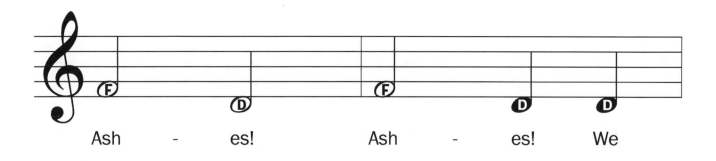

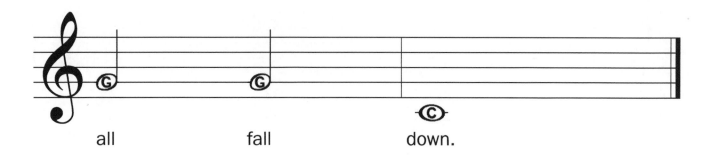

Baa Baa Black Sheep

English Folk Song

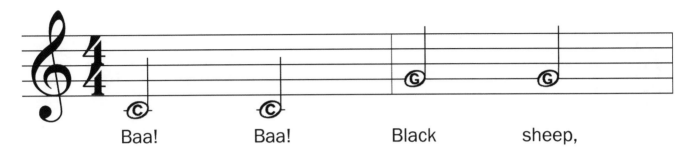

Baa!   Baa!   Black   sheep,

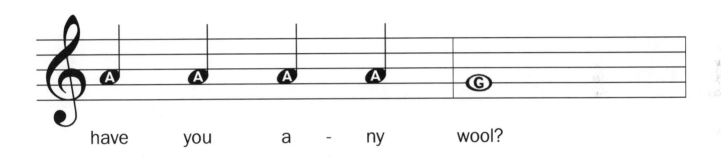

have   you   a - ny   wool?

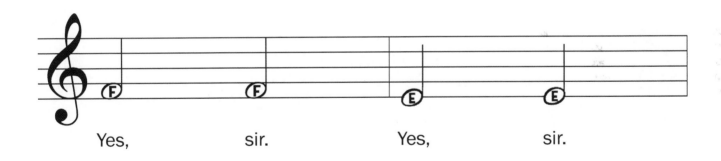

Yes,   sir.   Yes,   sir.

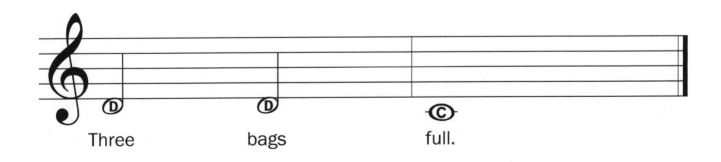

Three   bags   full.

Twinkle, Twinkle, Little Star

French Folk Tune with Lyrics by Jane Taylor

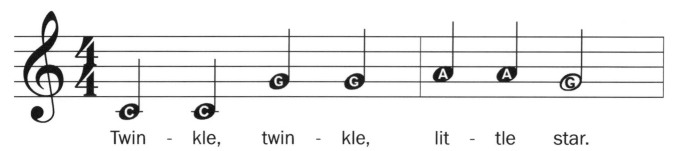

Twin - kle, twin - kle, lit - tle star.

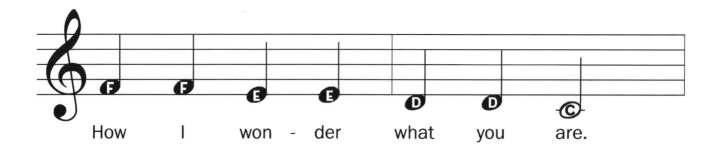

How I won - der what you are.

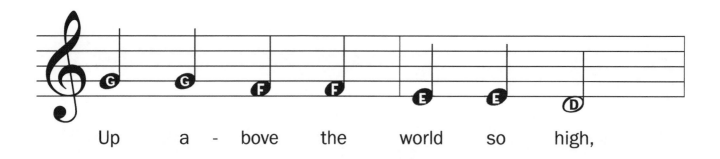

Up a - bove the world so high,

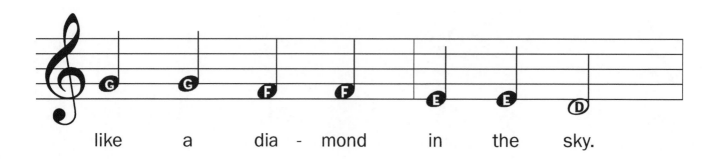

like a dia - mond in the sky.

Twinkle, Twinkle, Little Star

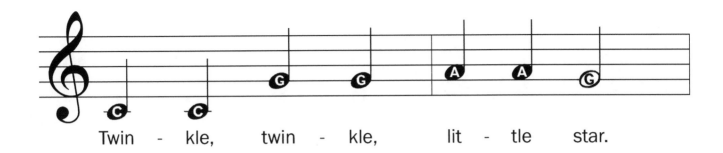

Twin - kle,   twin - kle,   lit - tle   star.

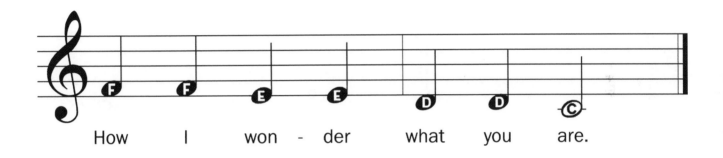

How   I   won - der   what   you   are.

For He's a Jolly Good Fellow

Folk Song from French Melody

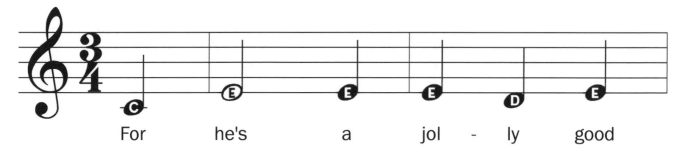

For he's a jol - ly good

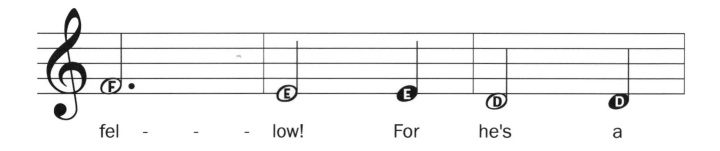

fel - - - low! For he's a

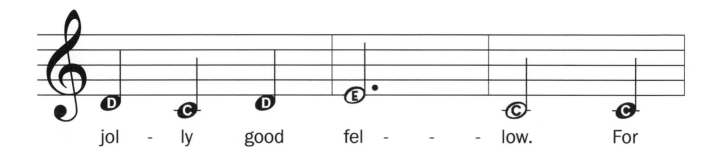

jol - ly good fel - - - low. For

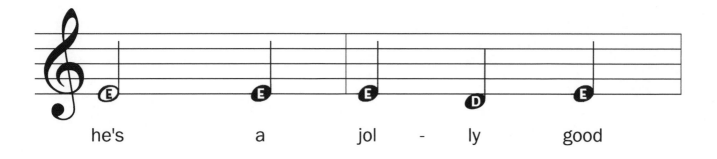

he's a jol - ly good

For He's a Jolly Good Fellow

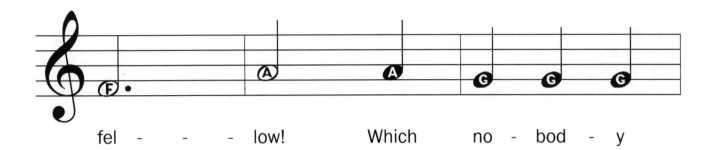

fel - - - low!   Which   no - bod - y

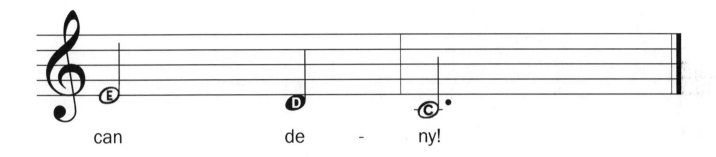

can   de - ny!

This Old Man

English Folk Song

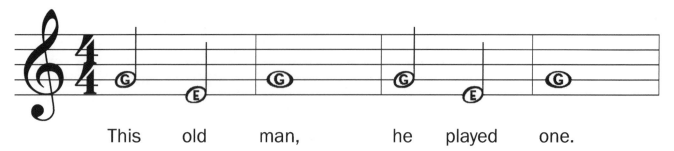

This   old   man,   he   played   one.

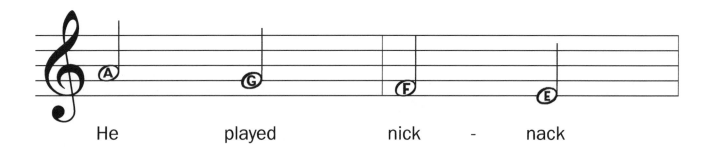

He   played   nick -   nack

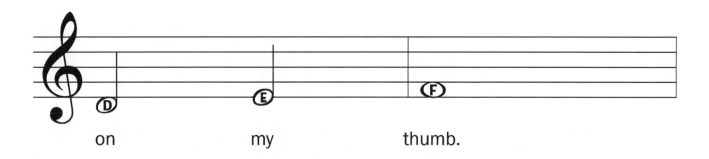

on   my   thumb.

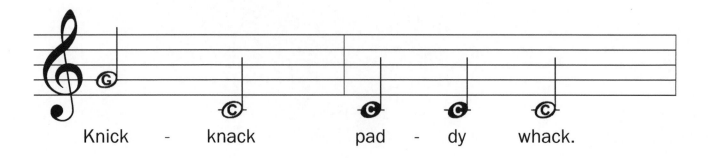

Knick - knack   pad - dy   whack.

This Old Man

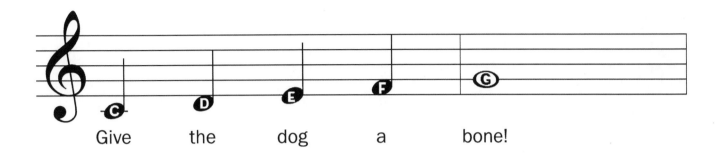

Give   the   dog   a   bone!

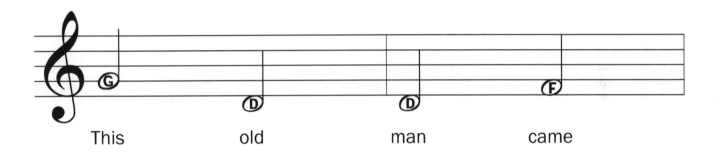

This   old   man   came

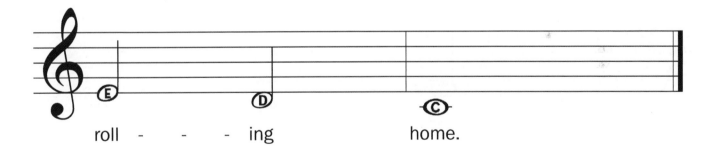

roll - - - ing   home.

Long, Long Ago

Thomas Haynes Bayly

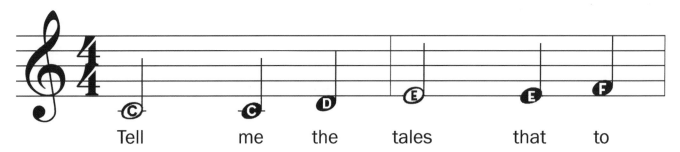

Tell   me   the   tales   that   to

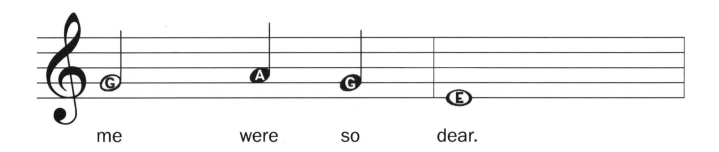

me   were   so   dear.

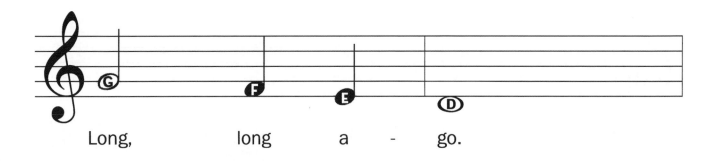

Long,   long   a - go.

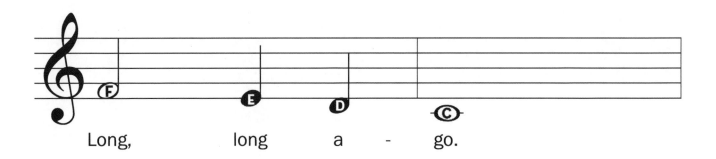

Long,   long   a - go.

Long, Long Ago

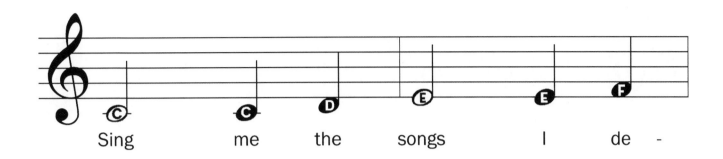

Sing   me   the   songs   I   de -

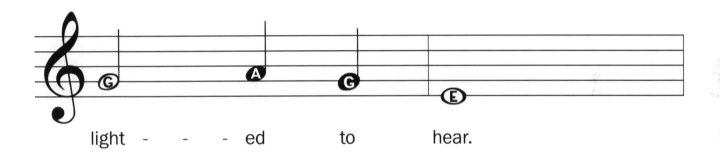

light - - - ed   to   hear.

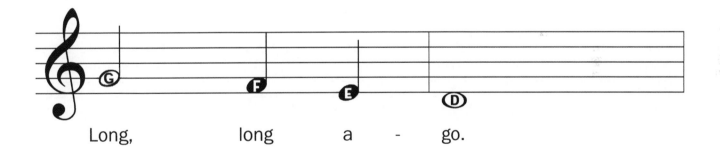

Long,   long   a - go.

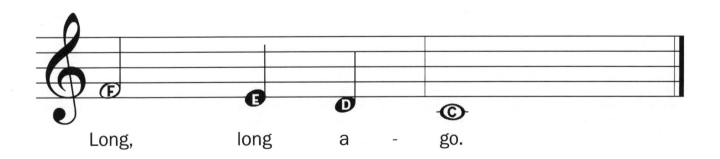

Long,   long   a - go.

Jolly Old Saint Nicholas

American Christmas Song

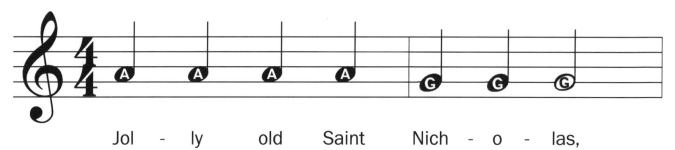

Jol - ly   old   Saint   Nich - o - las,

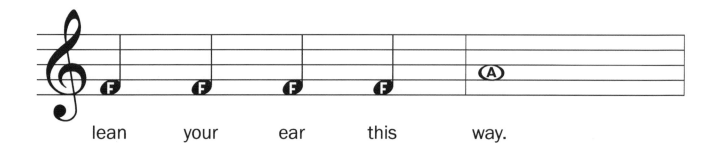

lean   your   ear   this   way.

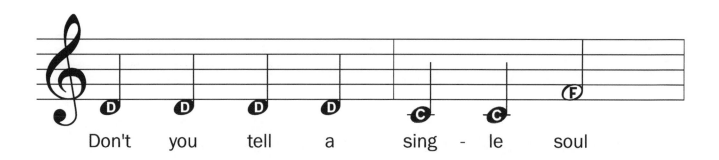

Don't   you   tell   a   sing - le   soul

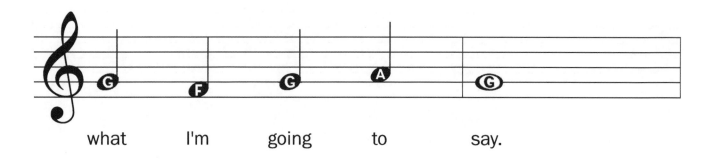

what   I'm   going   to   say.

Jolly Old Saint Nicholas

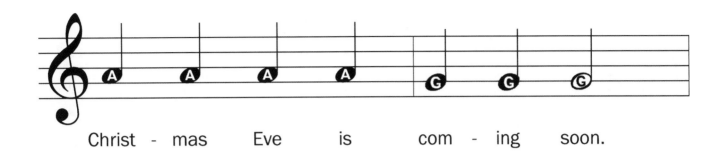

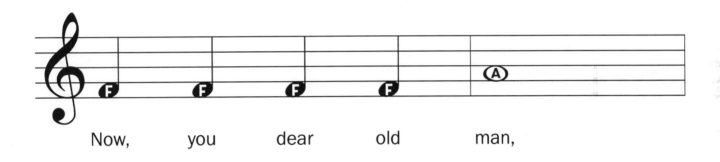

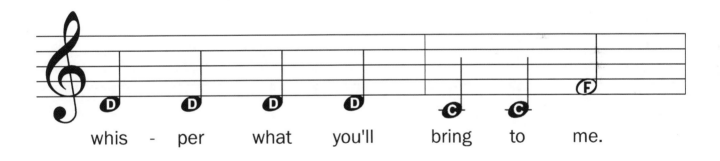

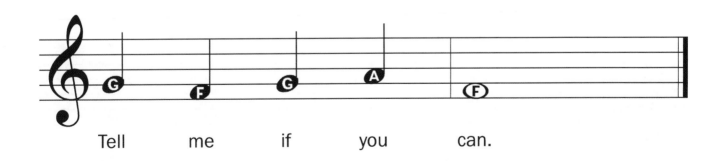

Lavender's Blue

English Folk Song

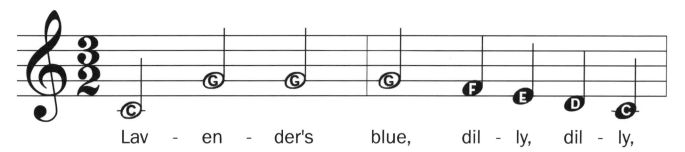

Lav - en - der's blue, dil - ly, dil - ly,

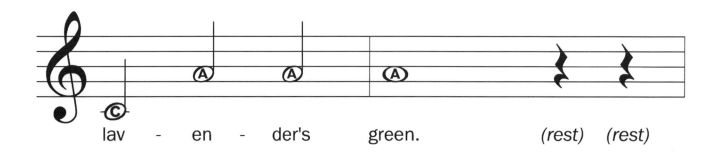

lav - en - der's green. *(rest) (rest)*

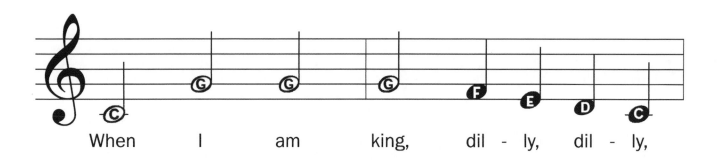

When I am king, dil - ly, dil - ly,

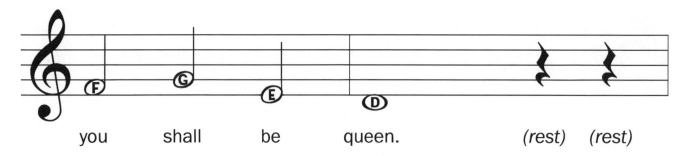

you shall be queen. *(rest) (rest)*

Famous Favorite
This song was used as the main musical theme
in Disney's 2015 version of *Cinderella*

Lavender's Blue

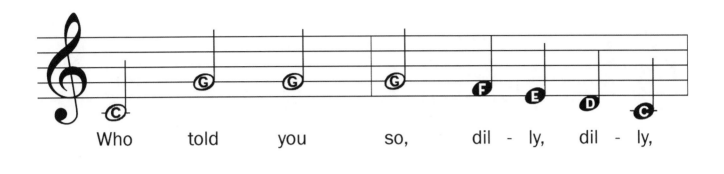

Who told you so, dil - ly, dil - ly,

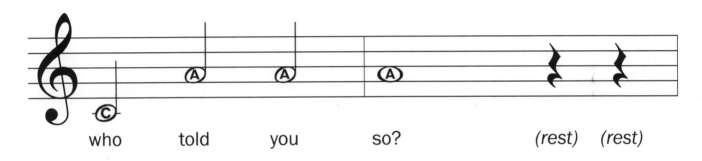

who told you so? *(rest)* *(rest)*

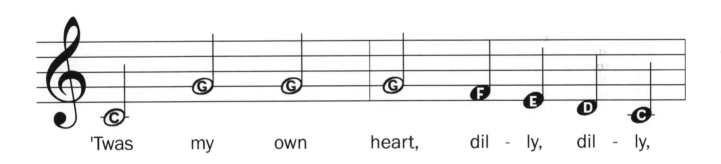

'Twas my own heart, dil - ly, dil - ly,

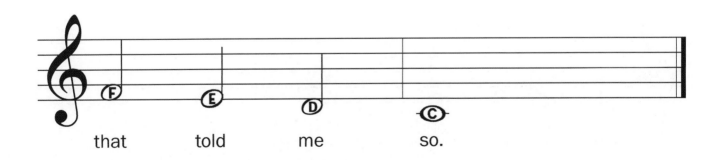

that told me so.

Skip to My Lou

American Folk Song

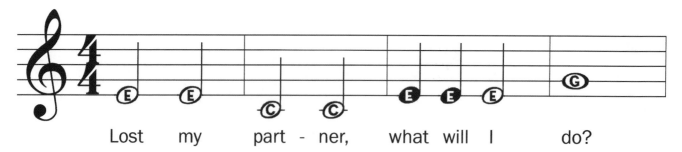

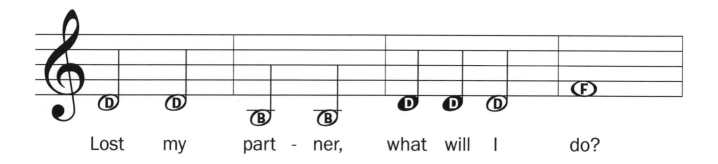

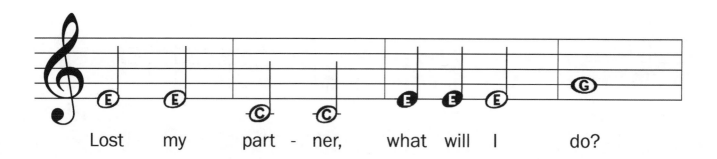

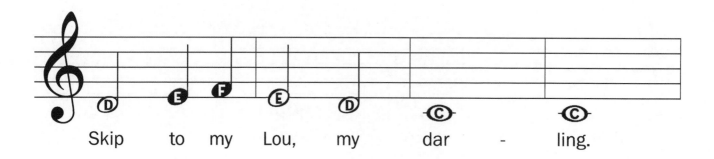

Skip to My Lou

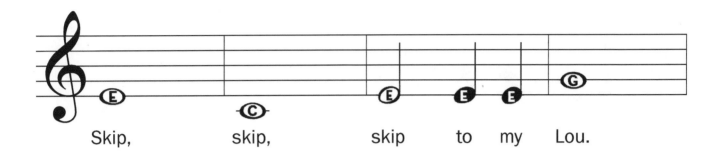

Skip,   skip,   skip to my Lou.

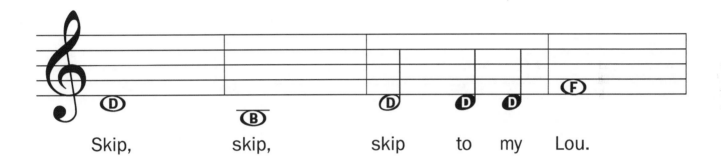

Skip,   skip,   skip to my Lou.

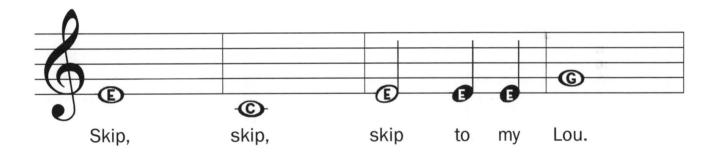

Skip,   skip,   skip to my Lou.

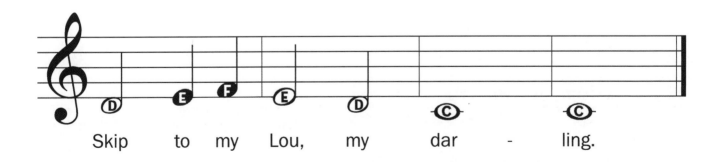

Skip to my Lou, my dar - ling.

Up on the Housetop

Benjamin Hanby

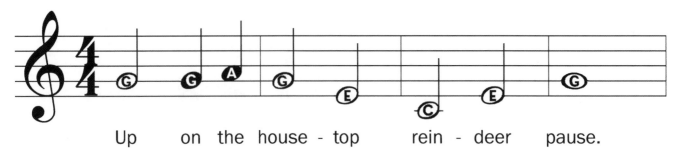

Up   on   the   house - top   rein - deer   pause.

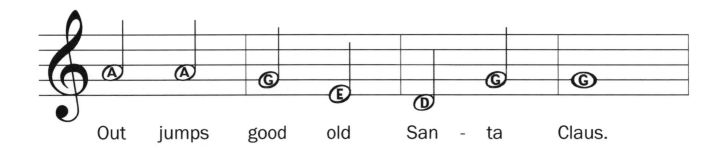

Out   jumps   good   old   San - ta   Claus.

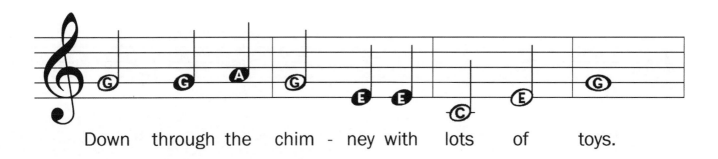

Down   through the   chim - ney with   lots   of   toys.

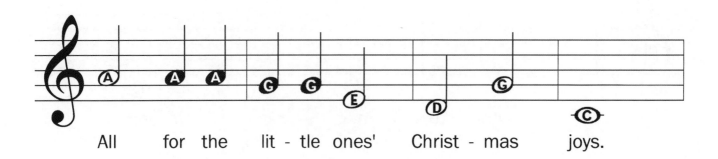

All   for   the   lit - tle ones'   Christ - mas   joys.

Up on the Housetop

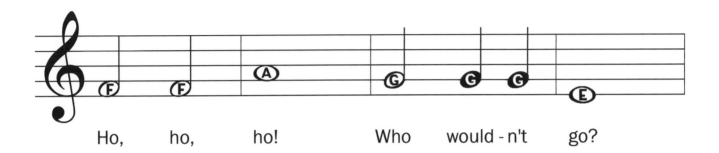

Ho, ho, ho! Who would-n't go?

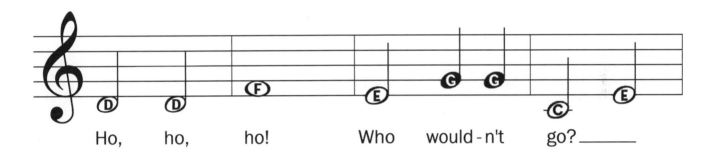

Ho, ho, ho! Who would-n't go? _____

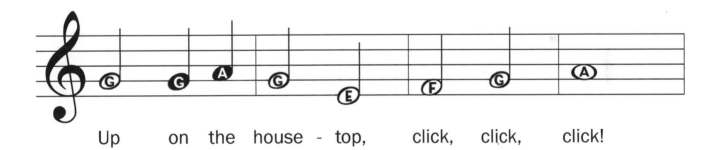

Up on the house - top, click, click, click!

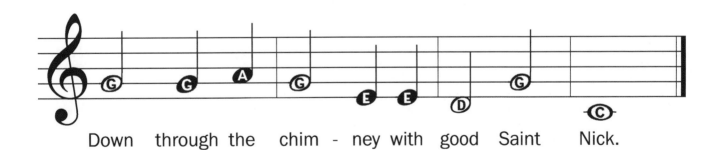

Down through the chim - ney with good Saint Nick.

Level Three

The songs in Level Three use both hands.

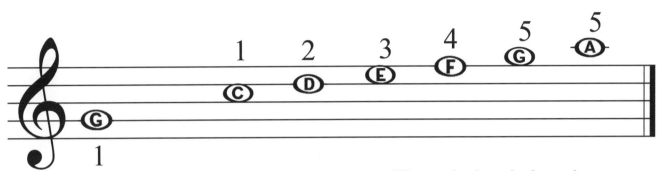

The left hand only
plays one note.

The right hand plays the same
notes, but sits higher to make
room for the left hand.

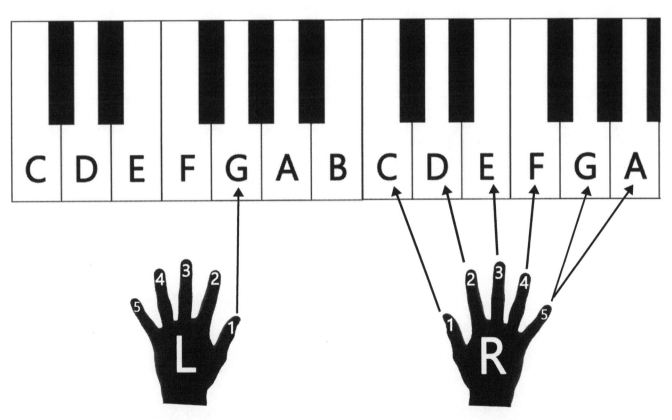

Find the G closest to the right hand and place your left thumb on it.

Are You Sleeping

French Folk Song

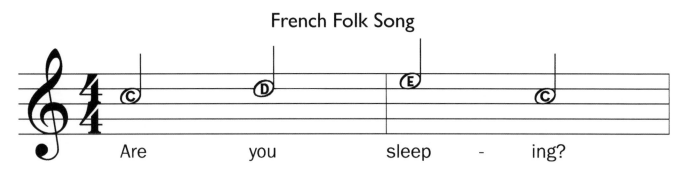

Are   you   sleep   -   ing?

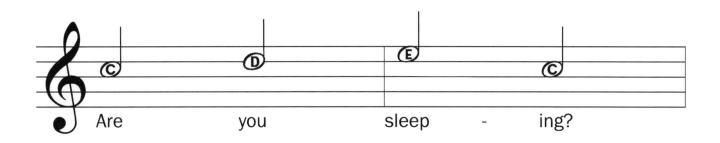

Are   you   sleep   -   ing?

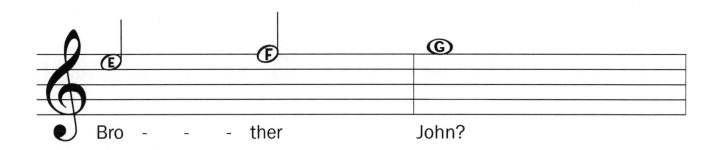

Bro   -   -   -   ther   John?

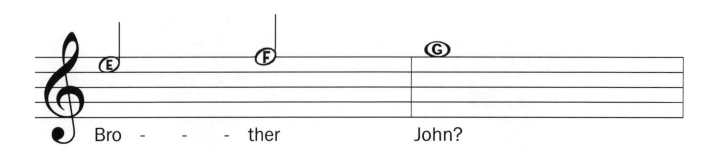

Bro   -   -   -   ther   John?

Are You Sleeping

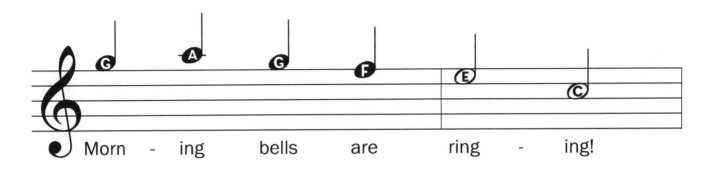

Morn - ing   bells   are   ring - ing!

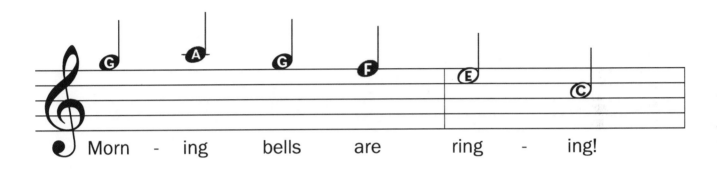

Morn - ing   bells   are   ring - ing!

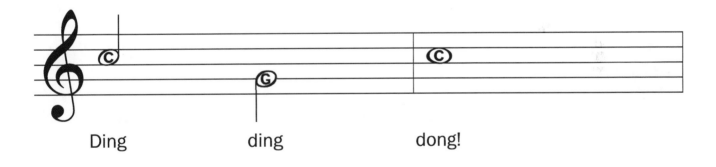

Ding   ding   dong!

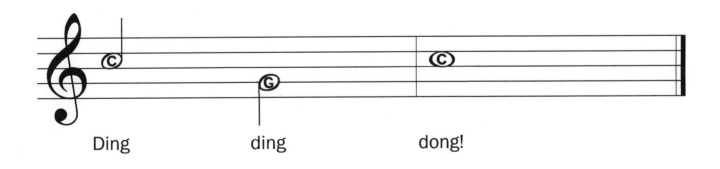

Ding   ding   dong!

55

Pop! Goes the Weasel

English Folk Song

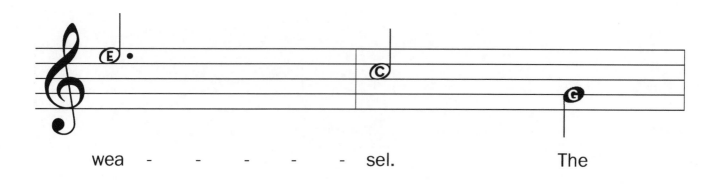

Pop! Goes the Weasel

Hush, Little Baby

American Folk Song

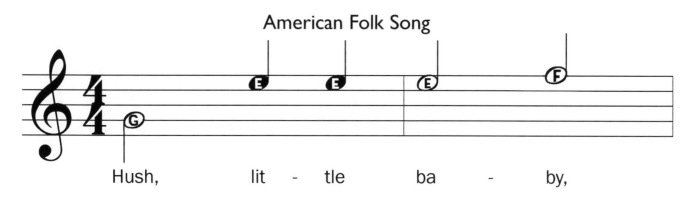

Hush,   lit - tle   ba - by,

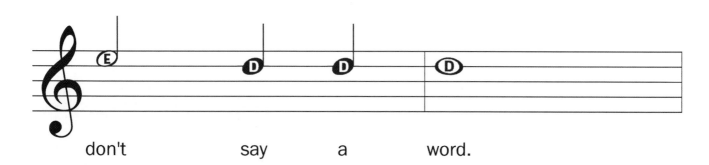

don't   say   a   word.

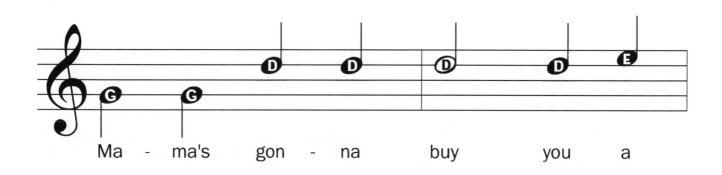

Ma - ma's   gon - na   buy   you   a

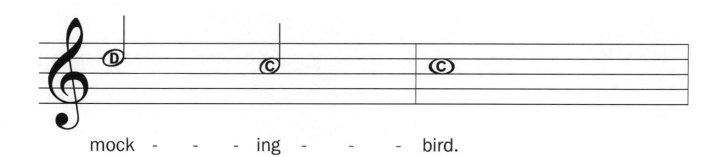

mock - - ing - - - bird.

Hush, Little Baby

The Farmer in the Dell

German Folk Song

The Farmer in the Dell

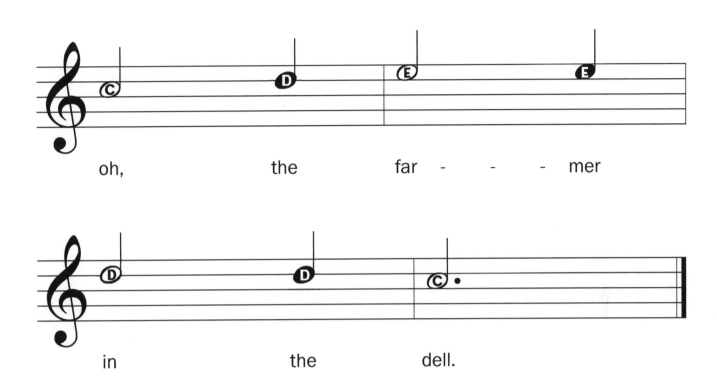

oh,   the   far -   -   -   mer

in   the   dell.

Rondeau

Jean-Joseph Mouret

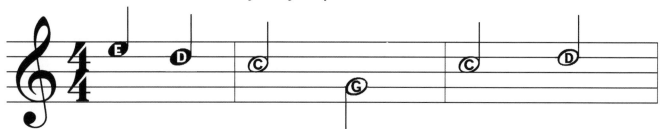

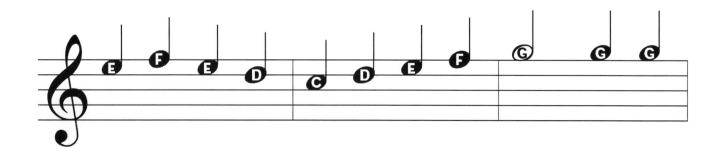

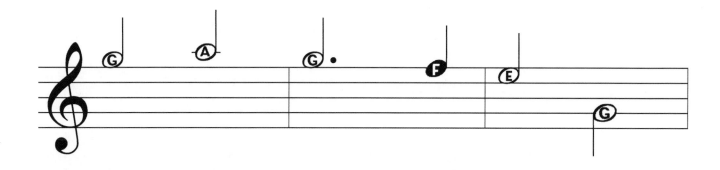

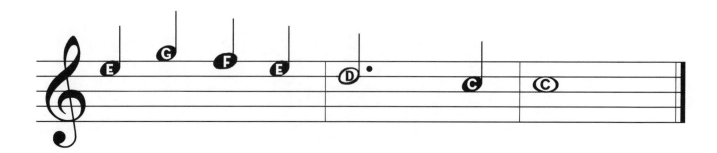

Famous Favorite
This tune is the theme song for the PBS
series Masterpiece Theater.

Alouette

French-Canadian Folk Song

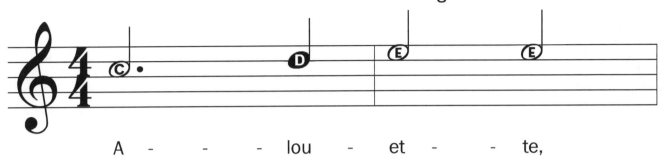

A - - - lou - et - - te,

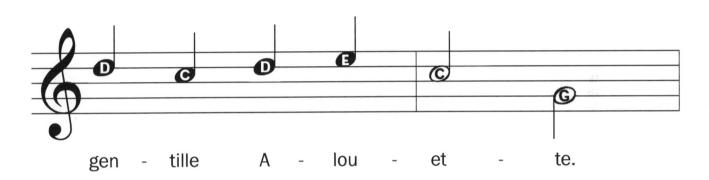

gen - tille A - lou - et - te.

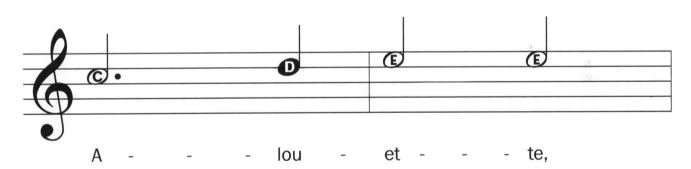

A - - - lou - et - - te,

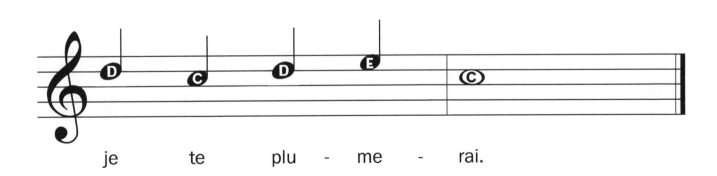

je te plu - me - rai.

Translation
Lark, nice lark.
Lark, I'll pluck your feathers.

Al Citrón

Mexican Folk Song

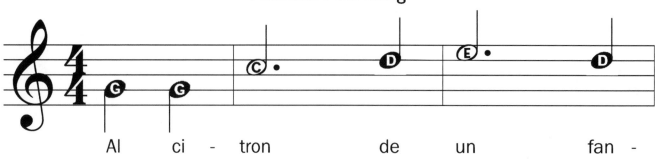

Al   ci - tron   de   un   fan -

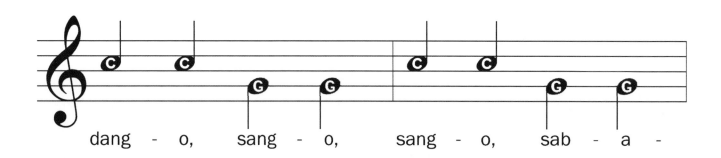

dang - o,   sang - o,   sang - o,   sab - a -

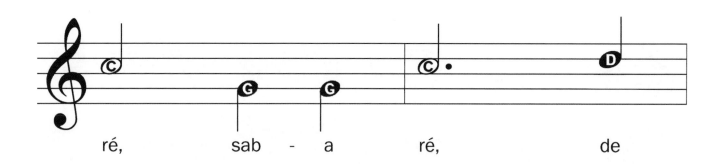

ré,   sab - a   ré,   de

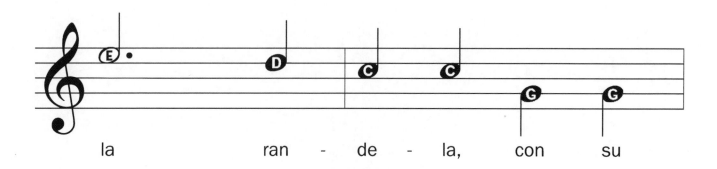

la   ran - de - la,   con   su

Translation
This song's lyrics are nonsensical and involve
citrus, dancing, and the sound of a rattling train.

Al Citrón

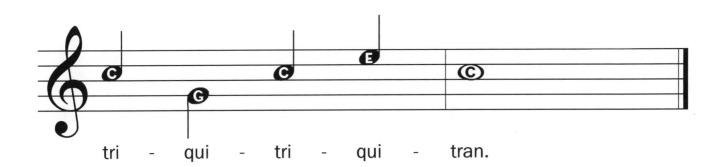

tri - qui - tri - qui - tran.

Level Four

The songs in Level Four use three left hand notes.

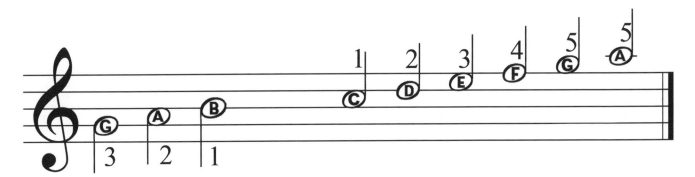

The left hand plays notes with the stem pointing down.

The right hand plays notes with the stem pointing up.

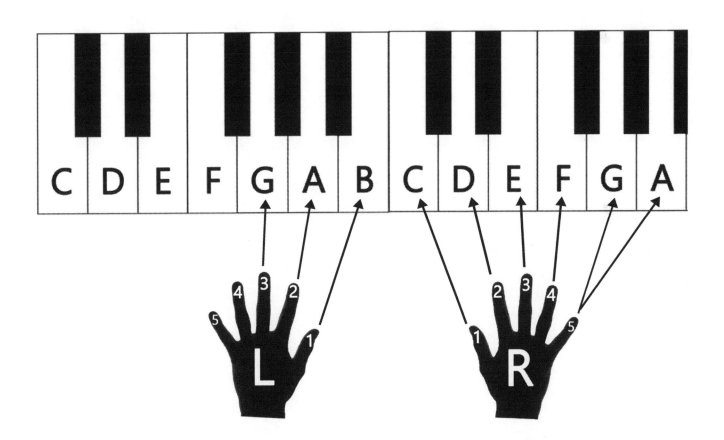

Your thumbs will sit beside each other on the keyboard.

For notes without a stem, use the notes around them as a guide, or check this chart to see which hand should play the note.

Yankee Doodle

American Folk Song

Yan - kee Doo - dle went to town

rid - ing on a po - ny.

Stuck a feath - er in his cap and

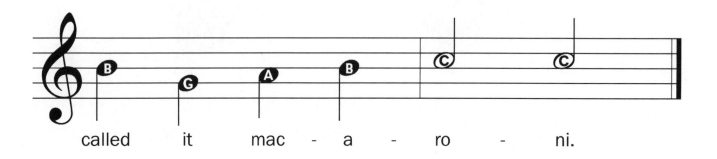

called it mac - a - ro - ni.

Happy Birthday

Patty and Mildred Hill

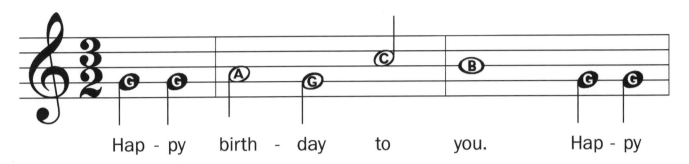

Hap - py   birth - day   to   you.   Hap - py

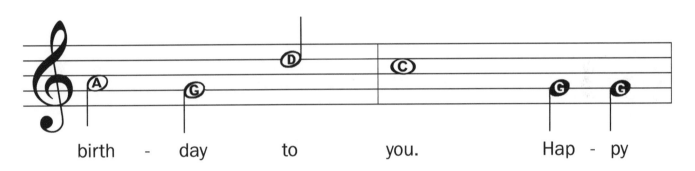

birth - day   to   you.   Hap - py

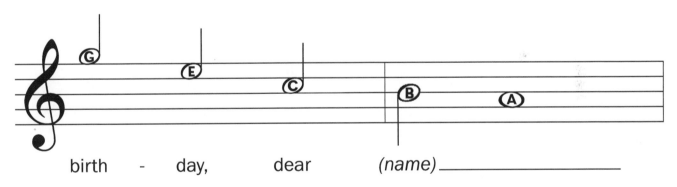

birth - day,   dear   *(name)* _____

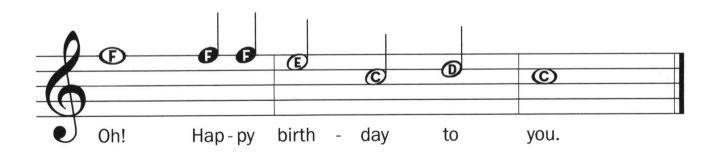

Oh!   Hap - py   birth - day   to   you.

The Muffin Man

English Folk Song

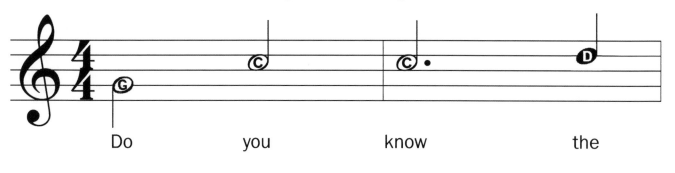

Do   you   know   the

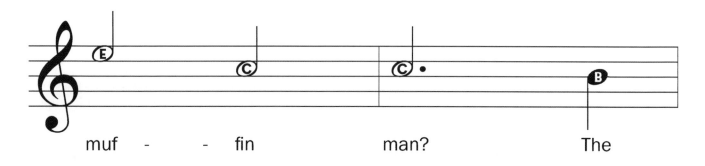

muf - - fin   man?   The

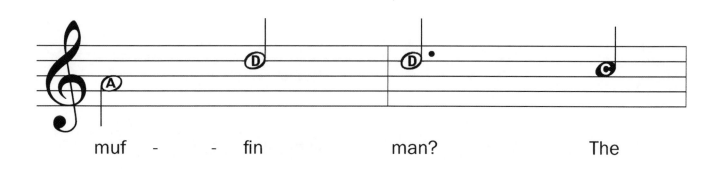

muf - - fin   man?   The

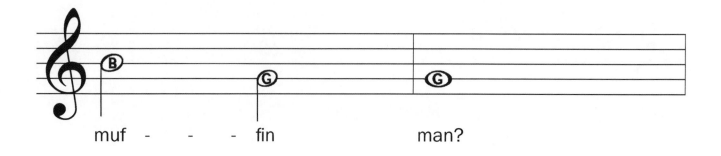

muf - - - fin   man?

The Muffin Man

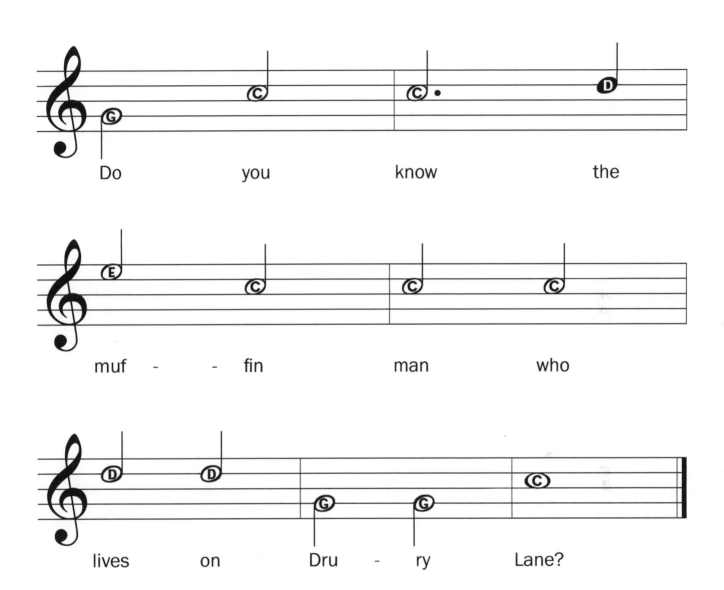

Old MacDonald Had a Farm

Folk Song

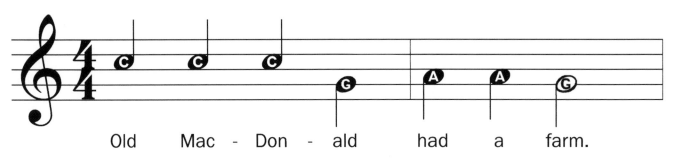

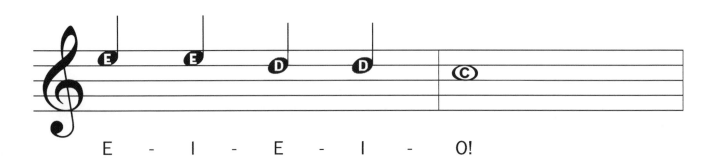

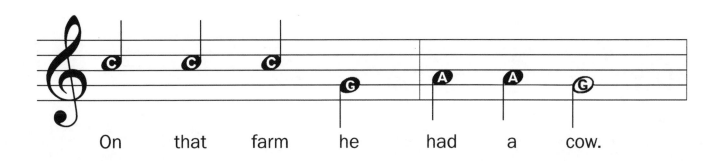

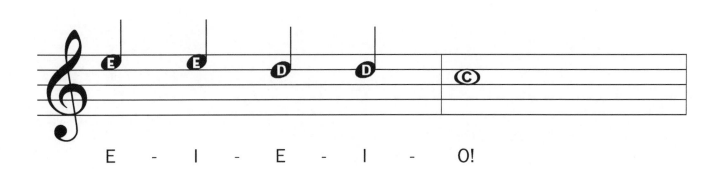

Old MacDonald Had a Farm

Home on the Range

Dr. Brewster Higley and Daniel Kelley

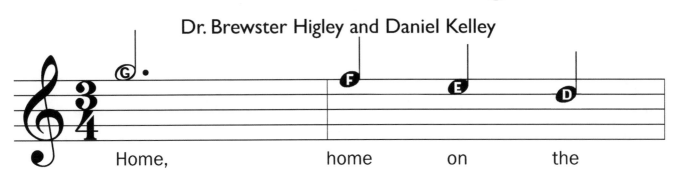

Home,   home   on   the

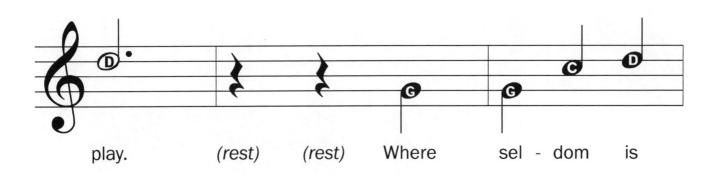

range.   *(rest)*   Where   the

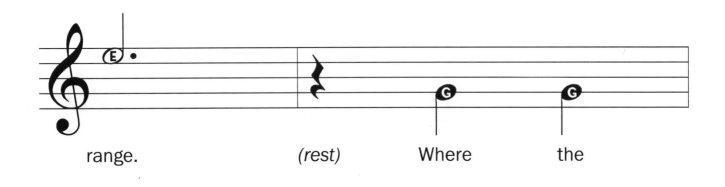

deer   and   the   an - te - lope

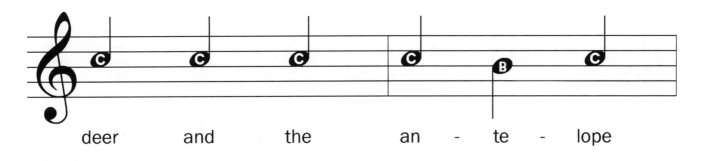

play.   *(rest)*   *(rest)*   Where   sel - dom   is

Home on the Range

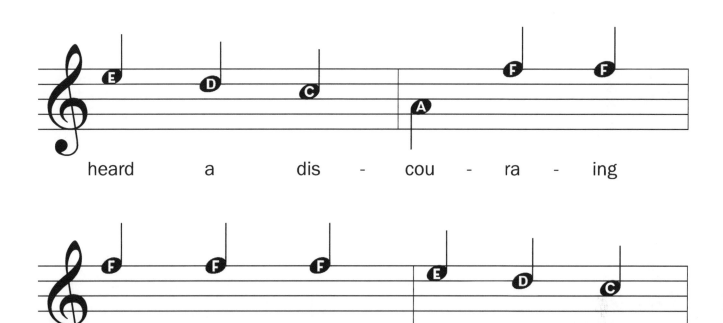

heard a dis - cou - ra - ing

word and the sky is not

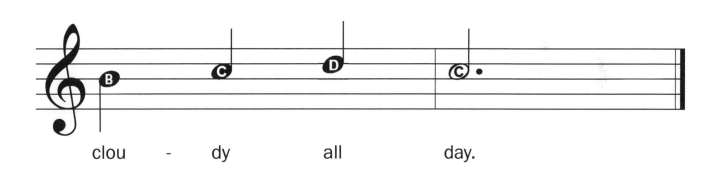

clou - dy all day.

We Wish You a Merry Christmas

English Christmas Carol

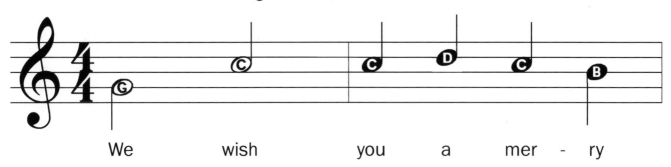

We   wish   you   a   mer - ry

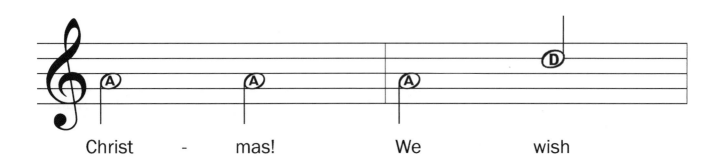

Christ - mas!   We   wish

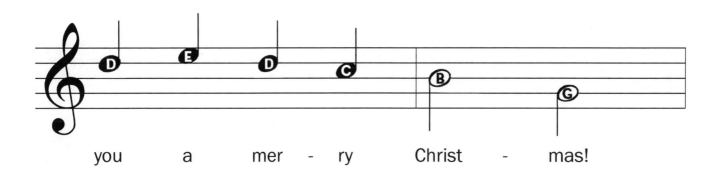

you   a   mer - ry   Christ - mas!

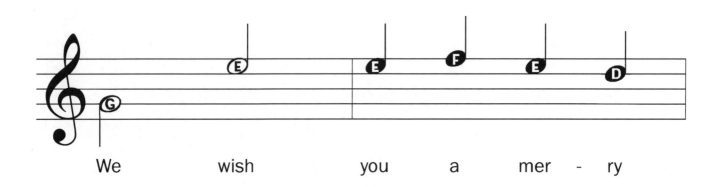

We   wish   you   a   mer - ry

We Wish You a Merry Christmas

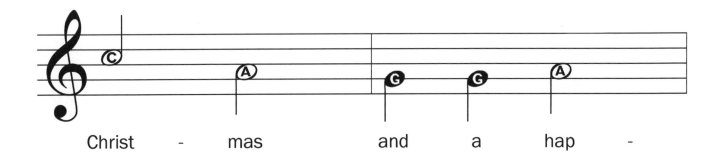

Christ - mas   and   a   hap -

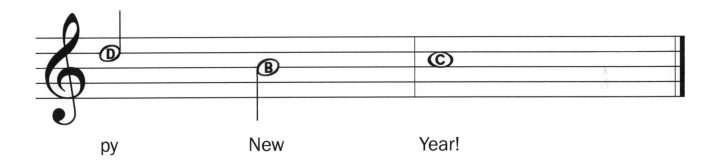

py   New   Year!

Down in the Valley

American Folk Song

Eine kleine Nachtmusik

Wolfgang Amadeus Mozart

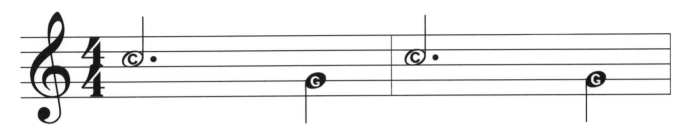

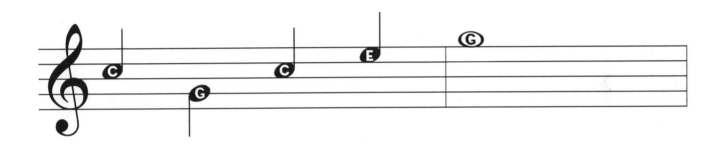

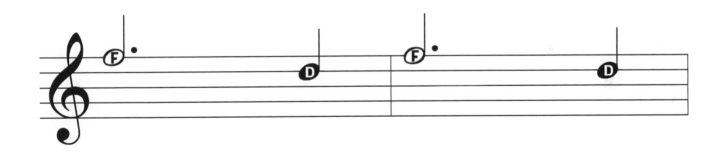

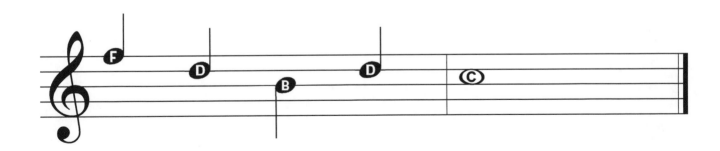

O Christmas Tree

German Christmas Carol

O   Christ-mas tree,   o   Christ-mas tree!   How

love - ly   are   your   bran - ches.   O

Christ-mas tree,   o   Christ-mas tree!   How

love - ly   are   your   bran - ches.

Surprise Symphony Theme

Franz Joseph Haydn

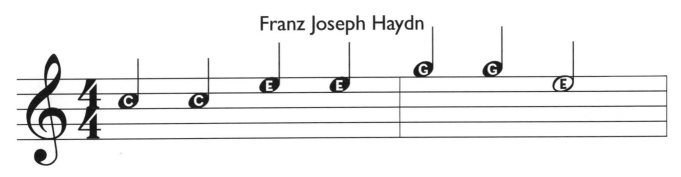

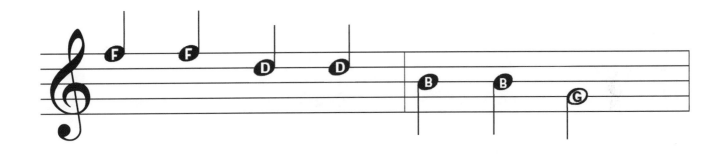

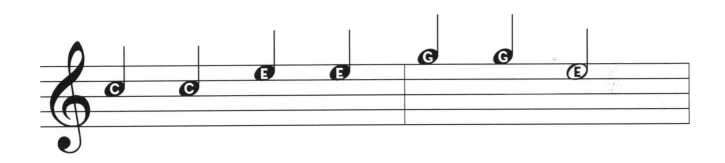

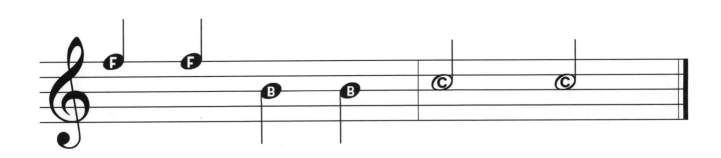

Amazing Grace

John Newton and E. O. Excell

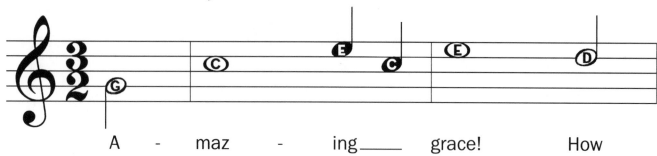

A - maz - ing___ grace! How

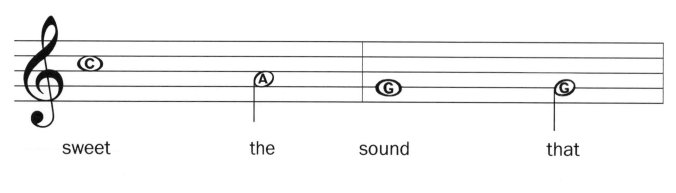

sweet the sound that

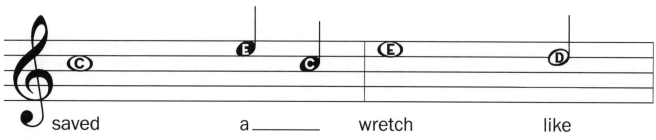

saved a___ wretch like

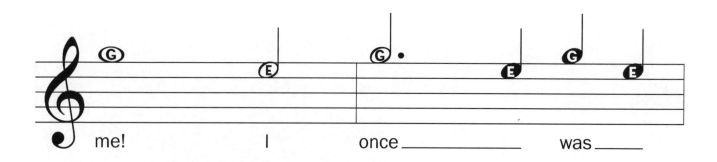

me! I once___ was___

Amazing Grace

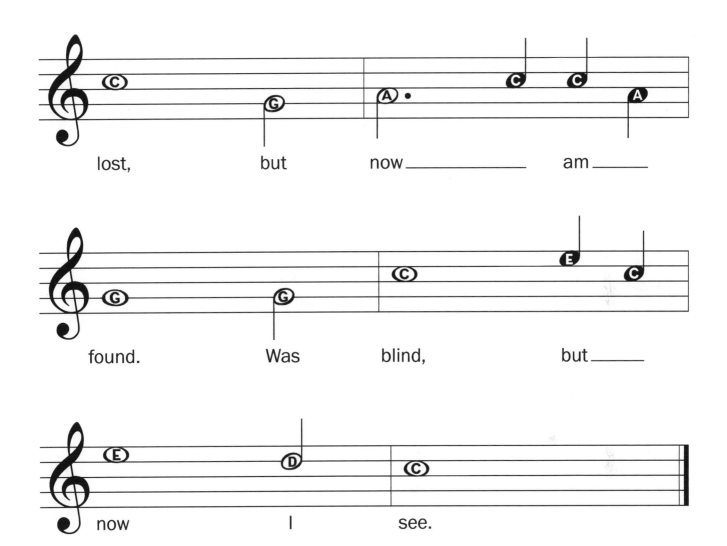

The Wheels on the Bus

American Folk Song

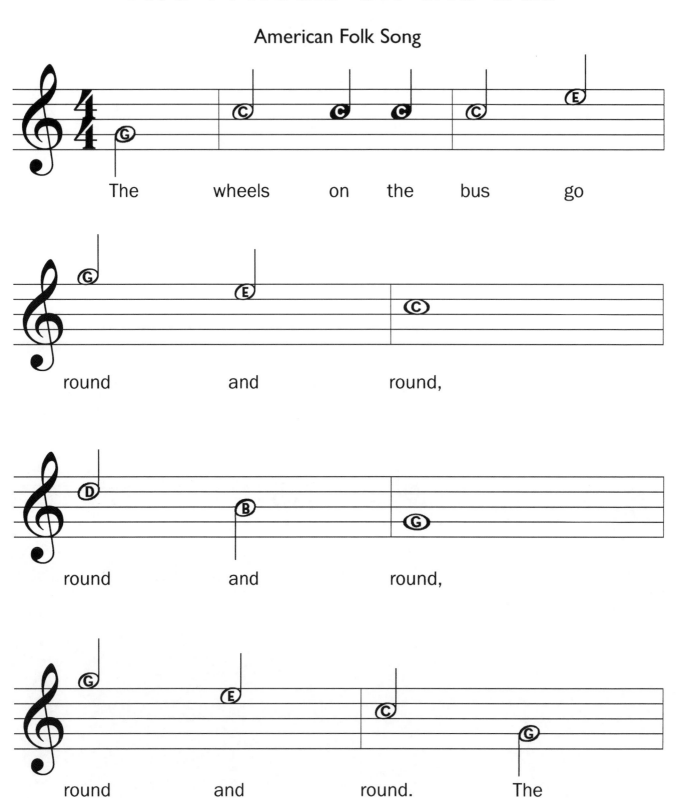

The Wheels on the Bus

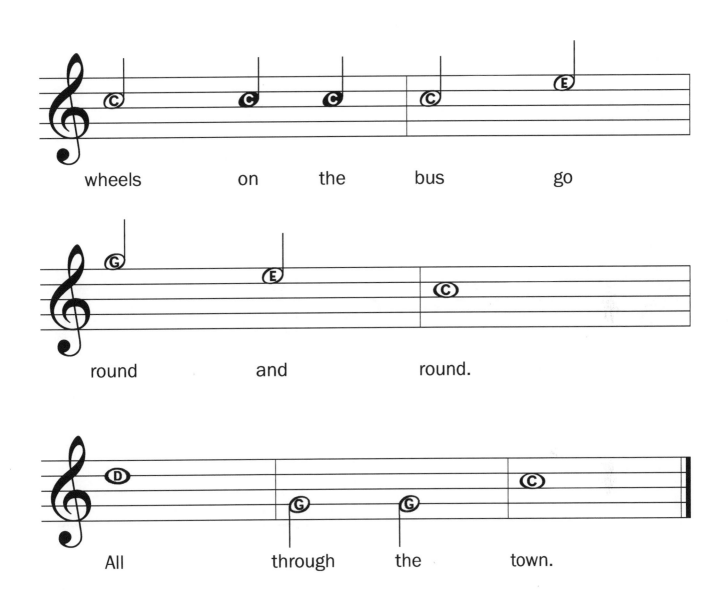

Bridal Chorus

Richard Wagner

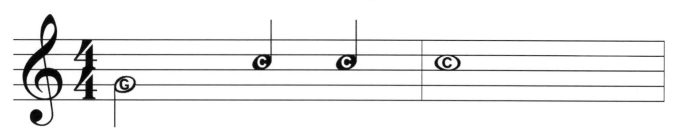

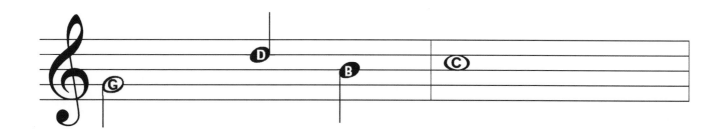

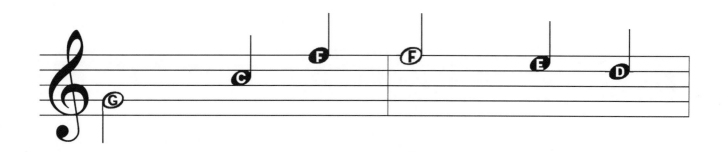

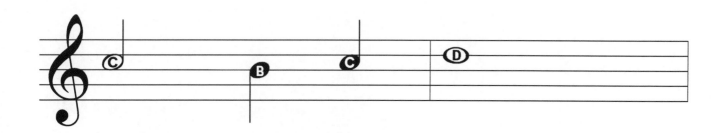

Bridal Chorus

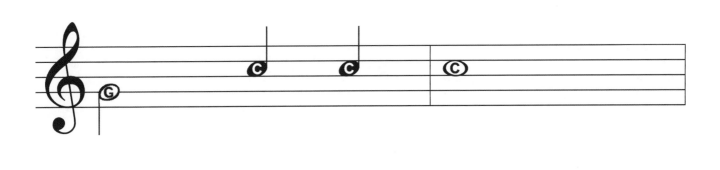

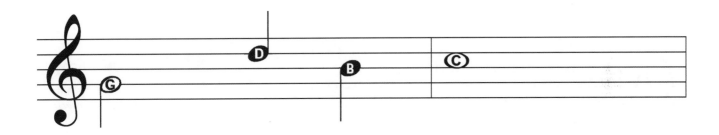

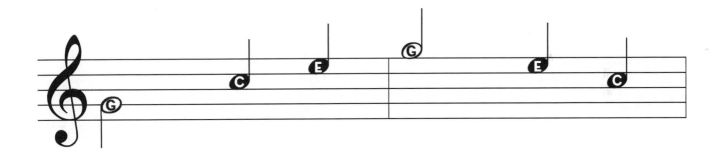

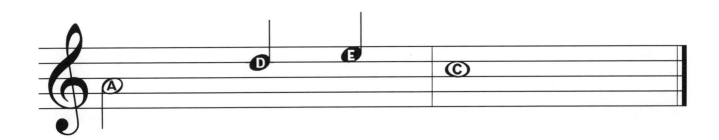

Korobushka

Russian Folk Song

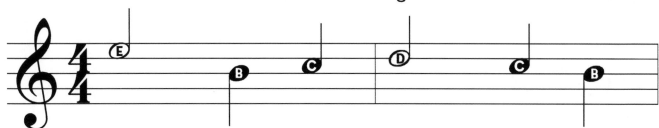

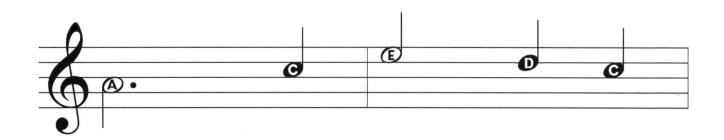

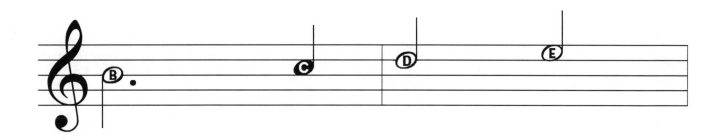

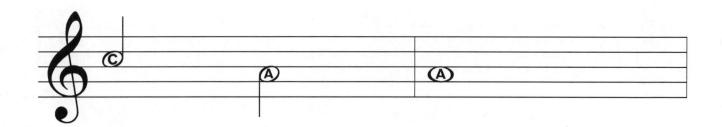

Famous Favorite
This popular tune was used as the main
theme in the first Tetris video game.

Korobushka

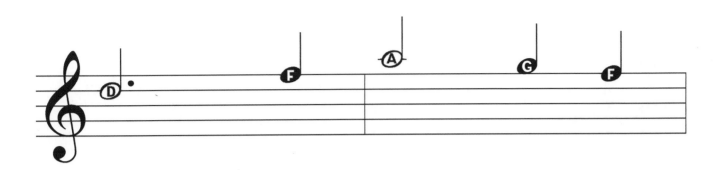

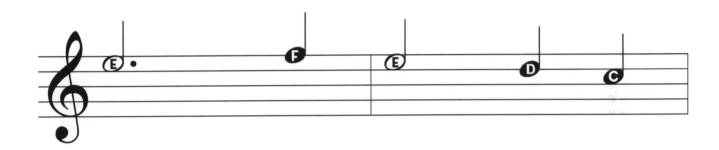

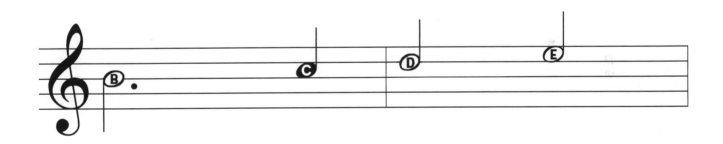

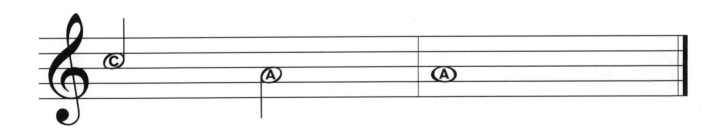

Scotland the Brave

Scottish Folk Song

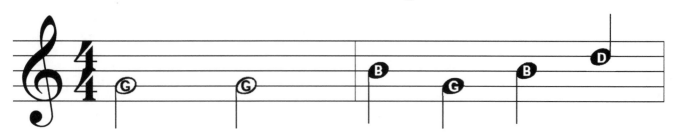

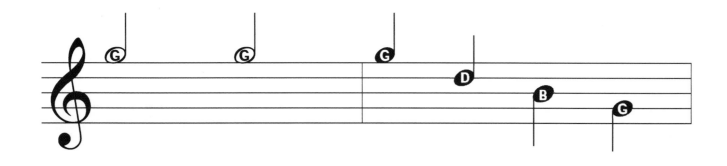

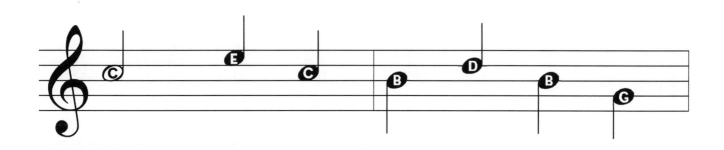

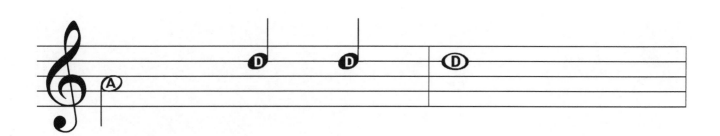

Scotland the Brave

William Tell Overture

Gioachino Rossini

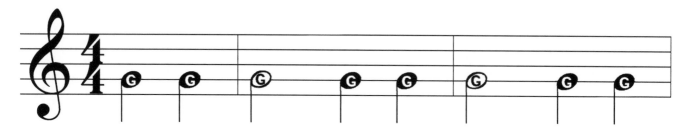

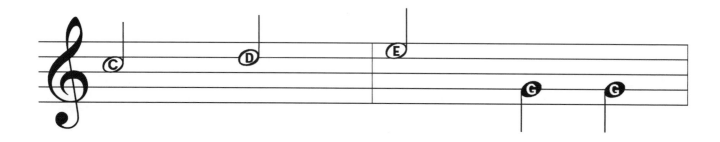

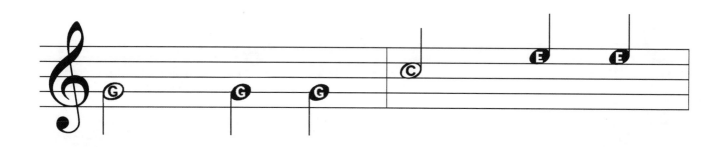

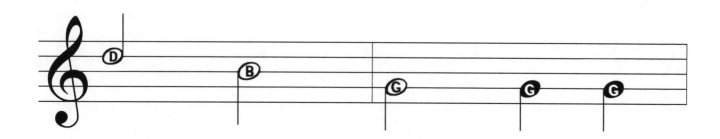

Famous Favorite
This song was used as the Lone Ranger's theme song
and has been featured in countless other productions.

William Tell Overture

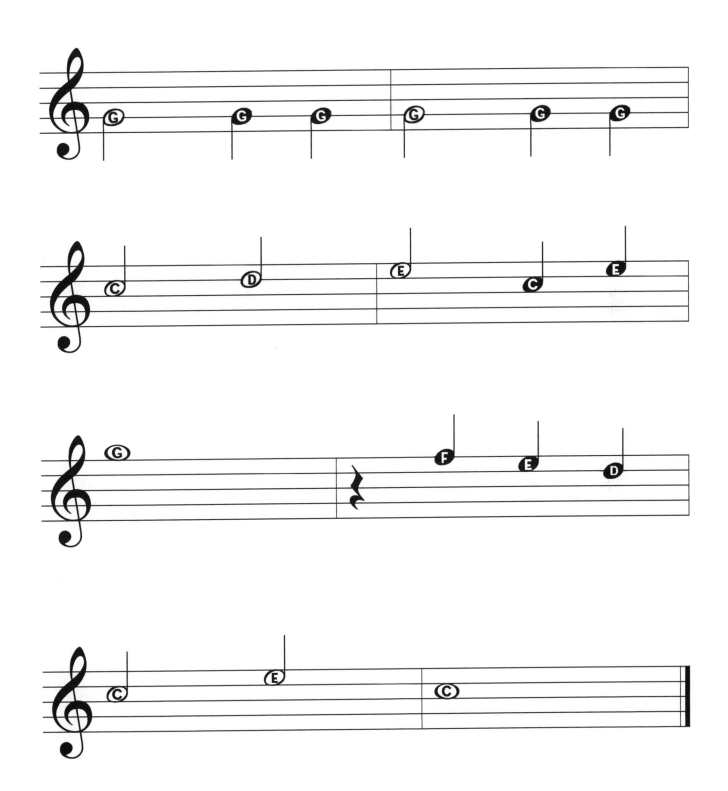

Bonus Downloads

This book includes free digital content.
Visit **www.avanellpublishing.com** or scan the QR code below
to access your bonus materials,

- Fully orchestrated recordings of each song

- Printable reference charts to use while you play

- Lessons and charts for left hand playing

- Practice tips to help you build your skills

- Sheet music of additional songs